D1258484

Good as Gold:

TECHNIQUES
FOR FUNDAMENTAL BASEBALL

FRANK WHITE
with MATT FULKS

Foreword by WILLIE RANDOLPH
Introduction by WHITEY HERZOG

SPORTS PUBLISHING L.L.C.
www.SportsPublishingLLC.com

SUSAN M. MOYER, Director of production

BOB SNODGRASS, Acquisitions editor

TRACY GAUDREAU, Project manager

JOSEPH BRUMLEVE, Dust jacket design

KIPP WILFONG, Developmental editor

HOLLY BIRCH, Copy editor

CHRIS VLEISIDES, Photo editor

©2004 Frank White
All rights reserved.

Photos provided by Chris Vleisides/Kansas City Royals except where noted.

Information for conditioning and nutrition chapter provided by Tim Maxey, strength and conditioning coordinator for the Cleveland Indians.

ISBN: 1-58261-741-4

DEDICATION

This book is dedicated to my dad, Frank Sr.,
for teaching me that to become a good baseball player, you have to have a
passion for the game, and you have to want to be the best.

This book is also dedicated to the players
who are working hard to learn the game's fundamentals.

Others on Frank White:

"(Frank's) certainly a good one to teach kids about fundamentals. … Much like Dave Concepcion in Cincinnati, Frank was the glue to the great Kansas City teams. … Frank was a great player with great hands, great ability. He was a smart player, and he could cover a lot of ground. He had great range. Those things are important for a middle infielder. He didn't necessarily make the headlines, but he did the things that it took to win. Teams win because they're strong up the middle. Frank certainly brought that to the diamond."
———*Ozzie Smith, Hall of Fame shortstop*

"I've always enjoyed talking to Frank about the game. It's obvious that he was a gifted player, but he changed some of the ways that second base was played. … He always was a student of the game. He took all of the little factors that were available to him and made himself better. I'm sure he has a lot to give about the craft of his position and the craft of baseball."
———*Cal Ripken Jr., Baltimore shortstop and future Hall of Famer*

"Had I not gone to spring training in 1982 — after making 47 errors in Jacksonville during my Double-A season — and watched Frank White field the ball differently than other infielders I had seen, I wouldn't have cut my errors to 17 the following season. To this day, that's how I teach infield play. I'm extremely grateful for learning that from Frank."
———*Buddy Biancalana, shortstop, who played next to Frank during the 1985 World Series*

"To see Frank emerge through hard work as one of the best — if not *the* best — defensive second basemen ever to play the game, it's special. Obviously, playing with him for all those years was a thrill, seeing him make all of those plays and accomplish the things he accomplished. Now, he's teaching new players what people have taught him. Frank's played, he's coached and managed, and he's spent a lot of time in the front office, including evaluating. So, he's touched all sides of the game of baseball. He's very qualified to write a how-to book on baseball."
———*George Brett, Hall of Fame third baseman and Frank's teammate during 1973-1990*

"I really think Frank's a good person to teach kids about the fundamentals of baseball. He had good mechanics as a hitter and as a defensive player. From base running to fielding to hitting, Frank was so fundamentally sound that he is excellent to teach the skills. I think the book will be well-received and will be something that kids can derive a lot of information from, and learn to play the game the right way."
———*Lou Piniella, longtime player and major-league manager*

"Frank was a great player; there's no question about that. I always enjoyed seeing him play. … He was a good clutch hitter who also could run and field. He could do everything. He had a great attitude and a lot of intelligence. Whatever you were looking for in a player, you found in Frank White."
———*Ernie Harwell, Hall of Fame broadcaster*

CONTENTS

FOREWORD

Willie Randolph

In the 1970s and early 1980s when I was playing with the New York Yankees, each player had at least one main rival with another team that we wanted to play at least as well as for that series. For catcher Thurman Munson it was Carlton Fisk; for third baseman Graig Nettles it was George Brett. Largely due to the fact that our teams met in some tough regular-season and playoff series, my main rival was Frank White. Our rivalry wasn't talked about as much in the media as some of the other more high-profile ones, but we knew it was there. That's what competition is all about—wanting to be the best on the field, making sure your team gets all the benefits that it can from you, but having respect for your opponent.

I think Frank and I always saw each other as the unsung heroes of our teams. Deep down inside we knew were just as important as the "big" guys. We played very similar roles on our ball clubs, and were proud of the roles that we played. We were counted on to do the little things to help our teams win, such as sacrifice bunting to move the runner into scoring position. We knew our roles and went about our business every day. As players, we would give each other a little nod before games because we knew that we were going to go hard at each other.

Watching Frank play motivated me. I always tried to pattern myself after his play and be as solid as he was defensively. It was frustrating to see some of the plays that he made only in the sense that we thought, "Darn, that son of a gun got us again." But he was so solid at second that we actually expected him to get us every now and again. His ability and attention to the fundamentals were motivating for me. I always wanted to one-up him, or at least be as solid as he was. We had a lot of respect for each other, and we still do.

We have always had a very quiet friendship, a bond really. Even though Frank was in Kansas City and I was in New York, he was very much a part of my career. Measuring myself against the best players at my position and seeing where I fit in with the other second basemen was a key to my success. I always wanted to play well against Frank so I could be toward the top of that list. Frank and I don't necessarily fit in the same category as Bill Russell and Wilt Chamberlain, but I can understand when Russell says he wouldn't have been the type of player he was without Wilt. I somewhat feel that way about Frank, because in all those years that we played against each other, we brought out the best in each other.

To this day, anytime we're in the same place, I seek him out, walk up to him and give him a hug. He kids me and calls me his idol, but I have to remind him that he's older than I am, so he should be my idol. We talk baseball, our families and our aspirations, because those are things that we've always had in common. There's just not a time when I'm in Kansas City or he's in New York

that we don't spend time together, even if it's just for a few moments to talk about the old days.

When I think about Frank White, besides him being a friend and a friendly rival of mine, solid, consistent defense is what comes to mind. I played against Frank for about 14 years, and one thing I admired was the defensive consistency he brought to the game every time he took the field. He was so smooth out there. His team could always count on him to make the tough play. Kansas City was very fortunate to have a solid middle infielder like Frank White to anchor those really good teams of the mid-1970s through the late 1980s. Those Royals teams had good pitching staffs and good hitters, but their defense was the key, and Frank was one of the main components to that group. People in baseball, people who know the game, know that Frank was a foundation of that club during some great winning years.

There were times when Frank moved a long way for a ball, stayed on balance, and made a strong throw to first to get a guy out. He made it look easy to the fans, but I would be in the dugout thinking, "Wow! That was a pretty tough play." As a fellow second baseman, I knew a lot of those plays weren't very easy because I was out there trying to do the same things. His soft hands and quick feet, which, to me, are the prerequisites for any really good infielder, were in sync in such a way that he could make a play look effortless. I enjoyed watching him play.

I always liked the way he turned the double play. I thought his double play was under control, very smooth and effortless. When the runner was charging down on him, Frank handled the pressure tremendously. People sometimes forget that when Frank and I played, we had to worry about runners coming hard into second base; today that isn't as much of a concern because of the rules. We had extra pressure turning the double play because that runner would try to knock us into left field.

When Frank asked me to write this foreword for *Good As Gold*, I was really flattered. I have always preached the fundamental aspects of baseball. I think it's important for kids to be taught the fundamentals to develop their game and to help them have fun as they move forward through their baseball careers. Those fundamentals are extremely important to Frank, too. He is a perfect example of practicing what you preach.

As a player, Frank made the fundamental plays consistently, which is the measure of a good middle infielder. That's what a team wants and what a team needs. He was so good at what he did that he made almost everything look easy. I remember some fancy plays that he made, but those aren't the ones that are important. Give me the player who's going to make the routine play day in and day out, and you can have all the fancy plays that you want—those aren't impressive to me. I want the player who's going to make the play when his team needs it, like in the bottom of the ninth inning with the bases loaded and one out, and he's able to turn the double play. That's what Frank brought to his teams.

When we see each other we often talk about the ways we're working with young major-league players on our teams—fundamental things that make players better, the proper way to do certain things—and it's great to hear his ideas. He knows how to work with a guy and explain how to become a better player. Having said all of that, there is no one better to teach kids about baseball fundamentals than Frank White.

When I was growing up, I remember reading Jackie Robinson's story, and a book on fundamentals by Gil McDougald, who was a good defensive player for the Yankees in the 1950s. I know if I was a kid coming up now, or a player trying to improve my game at any level, I would want to read an instructional book by Frank White. You just don't get any better than that. I'm sure that any player or coach who picks up this book will benefit from the experience.

ACKNOWLEDGMENTS

As with most books, there seems to be too many people to thank. However, the authors would like to recognize personally the following for their hard work, dedication and support during this project.

To Kipp Wilfong, Bob Snodgrass and the rest of the team at Sports Publishing for their patience, guidance and desire to make this the best instructional book ever.

To Tim Maxey, the Cleveland Indians' strength and conditioning coach, for helping make the conditioning chapter the best that it could be. To Chris Vleisides for taking great instructional photographs. To the Royals' Chris Stathos for helping secure additional photos. To Dan Glass and the Royals operations staff for encouragement and assistance throughout the book process. To Trevor Vance and his groundscrew at Kauffman Stadium for working around their schedules to accommodate ours.

To Jon Pattin, Jaime Bluma and the team at Old Ballgame Training Academy for allowing us to use your fantastic facilities.

To the Royals founder, the late Ewing Kauffman, who stressed the benefit of fundamental baseball and had the idea for the Royals Academy, which helped give me a chance to play major-league baseball.

To our photo "models"—T.J. Gerrity, Pat Maloney, Kevin Sears, David Snodgrass, Jonathan Williams, Josh Williams, Shawn Whitney. Whether in baseball or not, may each of you reach your dreams and goals in life.

To Jim Wissel for your friendship and assistance during the project.

To Willie Randolph and Whitey Herzog for your friendship and willingness to write the great foreword and introduction. To the current and former major leaguers who took time out of their schedules to offer their most difficult fundamentals and best advice for other players and coaches.

We each would like to thank our parents, brothers and extended families for their encouragement throughout our lives. Finally, Frank would like to thank his wife, Teresa, and children—Frank III, Adrianne, Terrance and Courtney, and stepsons Darryl, Michael, Jordan and Joseph Hurtt (both of whom also were models)—for being supportive throughout this project and his career. Matt would like to thank his wife, Libby, and children—Helen and Charlie—for their support, understanding and putting up with his Elvis quirks during this book.

Thank you all.

INTRODUCTION

Whitey Herzog

During my managerial career I was fortunate to have two players who were supposed to be great with a glove but not with a bat; however, they each made themselves good hitters: Ozzie Smith in St. Louis and Frank White in Kansas City. When I arrived in Kansas City in 1975, the big knock on Frank was that some people didn't think he had the intestinal fortitude to hit and that he was afraid at the plate. I heard that time and time again. I never believed it for a second. By the end of Frank's career he had become a clean-up hitter and proved to be a good clutch hitter with power.

I have to say that the way he worked at the game, not only defensively but also offensively, he made himself the ballplayer that he was. Frank had a lot of natural talent on defense, and he worked at becoming a good hitter. We had a tough infield in Kansas City with Freddie Patek at shortstop, George Brett at third base and Frank at second base. From that experience, I can say that Frank White was the best defensive second baseman I have ever seen. Hands down! There are four things you want a second baseman to do: go left, go right, come in, and go out. Frank could do those four things better than any second baseman I have ever seen. Then when you talk about his vertical jump, you're talking about something else he could do better than any second baseman I have ever seen; and I've seen second basemen who were pretty darn good, such as Bobby Richardson and Bill Mazeroski. Frank played second base for me for five years, and I just don't see how you play the position defensively any better than he played it. Simply put, Frank was an extremely talented defensive player.

If Frank had played for the New York Yankees, that town never would have heard of Willie Randolph. Willie was a fine player, don't get me wrong, but I don't think he was as good as Frank defensively. (In fairness to Willie, he was a .280 hitter from day one.) There's no doubt in my mind that if Frank had played in a market like New York, or had we gone to the World Series in

Kansas City in the 1970s, he would be in the Baseball Hall of Fame. Frank made so many great plays during his career—and he made tough plays look easy—that it's tough to remember a lot of them. In the fifth and deciding game of the 1977 American League playoffs against the Yankees, however, Frank made a play that I will always remember. We were leading 3-2 in the eighth inning with two outs. Reggie Jackson was on first and Chris Chambliss was at the plate. Chambliss hit the ball up the middle, and Frank made an incredible diving stop, threw the ball to Freddie covering second to force out Jackson and

end the inning. That was an incredible play that gave us a chance to win the game. Nobody ever mentions that play because we ended up losing the game and the series. Still, it was one of the best plays I have ever seen in my life. Frank was just a uniquely gifted athlete.

The bad part about managing a player like Frank is that you take for granted that he's going to make all the tough plays, and probably make them look pretty easy. Sometimes it was easy to overlook the great things he did on the field. I've been fortunate to manage some great players, especially at middle infield. Frank White and Freddie Patek in Kansas City, and Tommy Herr with Ozzie Smith in St. Louis are two of the best double-play combinations in the history of the game. With a man on first, as a manager you'd want the ball to be hit on the ground. You knew that one of those guys was going to suck it up and they would get two outs. The great thing about managing a player like Frank is that he was a very easy player to work with. I had no problems with him. He was ready to play all the time. Frank just wanted to be in the line-up. Fundamentally, Frank was a very sound player. He definitely did a whale of a job for us.

They say great players can't teach, but that doesn't apply to Frank. He coached at the major-league level for several years, and I've heard a lot of good comments about him as an instructor. I strongly believe that he has the knack for teaching players at any level how to play baseball the proper way.

Chapter 1

Introduction to Good As Gold Play

Baseball is the greatest game in the world. In what other sport do you have an opportunity to be great at a multitude of things to help your team win? Baseball is it.

This book is about developing a full understanding and enjoyment of the game, to the point that you want to be good in every phase of it. Learning baseball's fundamentals will give you a good understanding of what the game's all about. That's why you should read this book.

Good As Gold is not just about hitting, and it's not just about pitching. It's about being a complete player and having an overall enjoyment of playing baseball. If you're a good hitter but a poor fielder, for instance, you're not going to enjoy all the phases of the game. As a true player, you want to be good at defense. You want to be a good hitter. You want to be a good base runner. You want to be a good thrower. If you neglect any of those areas, then you are not really enjoying your career as a baseball player as much as you could.

For young players, it's just as great to get a good hit as it is to make a great defensive play. One thing that little kids love to do in baseball is slide. They love to hit one in the gap and be able to run the bases properly in order to slide into third base with a triple. That's an awesome feeling! That's what this book is about.

DEFINING FUNDAMENTALS

The term "fundamental baseball," which you'll see throughout the book, to me means being the best fundamentally sound player that you can be. Be a good hitter. Be a good base runner. Be a good defensive player. Be a smart player. Be a player who thinks through a possible situation before the ball is pitched. Be a good team player.

Concentrating on baseball's fundamentals is no different than any task that you undertake. In any task, you have to learn the basics to be good at it. You should try to be as perfect an all-around player as you can be.

Baseball requires you to think. Unlike most sports, baseball has no playbook. In baseball, you have to pre-think the play before it happens. On every pitch, you need to know what you're going to do if the ball is hit in your direction. Then, when the ball is hit you can react to that situation. If the ball is hit before you pre-think the play, you may not have time to react.

To be a good all-around player, you need to be a good thinker (see chapter 7). I don't feel that many players make enough of an effort to be the best thinkers on the field. Many players go on the field and hope things happen, instead of going out there and making things happen.

There are three types of baseball players: those who watch things happen; those who make things happen; and those who say, "What happened?" The ones in the last group don't last too long. I want you to have the tools and the mentality to last as long as you can in this game.

LEARNING THE FUNDAMENTALS

Everybody has to go through a process to learn how to play baseball both physically and mentally, with proper fundamentals. Regardless of how good you think you are—and you might have outstanding abilities—you can improve at least one aspect of your game fundamentally. Part of what makes baseball such an interesting sport is that you can be a remarkable athlete and succeed with your natural ability or you can be an average athlete and succeed with strong fundamentals.

The ease, or difficulty, with which a player can learn—or a coach can teach—fundamental baseball depends largely on the individual. Simply reading and applying what you learn from this book will not transform you into a major-league prospect. I can't even guarantee that you'll become a superb defensive player or a feared hitter. However, I can guarantee that the teachings of this book can make you a better player and help you reach your full potential in this great game. Your talent level will dictate how quickly you pick up these ideas and analyze the areas of your game that need improvement. Becoming a better player also will take work and dedication. You can do it.

MY BEST ADVICE

"Former Pittsburgh Pirate manager Chuck Tanner told me one time that we're all born with a certain amount of ability. It might be a small circle or it might be an enormous one. But, until you become fundamentally comfortable with your own ability, Tanner said, you build confidence. When the confidence comes, you become somewhat bored and start to work on the perimeter of that circle. And, son of a gun, if that circle doesn't start growing… Just because you can't hit as far as Mark McGwire or field like Frank White doesn't mean that you can't have a long career in baseball. With fundamentals, you can play this game for a long time. Players sometimes have a hard time realizing that."

—*Tony Muser, former big-league player and current coach at the major-league level. I was coaching in Kansas City when he was the manager there, and I know the importance he places on fundamentals.*

WHY ME?

Learning baseball's fundamentals was one of the biggest keys to helping me enjoy a long career in the game. When my playing career ended with the Kansas City Royals in 1990, I knew immediately that I wanted to somehow teach the game of baseball and apply what I learned as a player. That chance came with the Boston Red Sox organization. I managed their Gulf Coast Rookie League team in 1992, before joining the big-league club for three years (1994-96) as their first base coach. I rejoined the Royals in 1997 in the same capacity, which included serving as the first base coach, the base running coach, and the outfielder's coach. After the 2001 season, I moved up to the front office as a special assistant to the general manager, Allard Baird, with responsibilities to assistant general manager Muzzy Jackson and team president Dan Glass. I was involved in various aspects of the club, but the bulk of the job included scouting and evaluating players and coaches. In 2004, I moved back to the field, managing the Royals class AA team in Wichita, Kansas.

Like many boys, my love of baseball began early in life with my dad. That love grew throughout my childhood in a neighborhood where you could find a pick-up game all summer. When baseball was in season, we were out there playing. I started playing the game when I was about nine years old. I really wasn't taught how to play baseball, though. Like most young players, I just wanted to get out there and play.

My high school didn't have a baseball team, but I played in various summer leagues throughout my high school years. I joined the Royals organization as a player after a successful tryout for their experimental baseball school called the Baseball Academy. As players in this program, we were drilled on playing baseball properly. We worked on fundamentals all afternoon, six days a week. In fact, we worked on fundamentals before we played games. (I proudly say that in 1973 I became the first "graduate" of the Academy to make it to the major leagues.)

MY BEST ADVICE

"When Frank came up to the majors, he had a lot of talent but he wasn't dripping with it. A lot of his longevity came from learning the game's fundamentals and working at them. A lot of players don't understand that philosophy… Too many bad things happen when your house is built on sand. Fundamentals are the foundation of your baseball career. That's how important they are. Frank understood that idea as a young player and applied those fundamentals."—*Tony Muser*

Through a ton of hard work and perseverance, I enjoyed a successful 18-year career with the Royals from 1973 to 1990. I took a lot of pride in being known as a strong defensive player, winning eight Rawlings Gold Glove Awards at second base. During my career, which spanned 2,324 major league games, I had a lifetime batting average of .255 with more than 2,000 hits, and the high honor of hitting cleanup for our 1985 world championship team.

Teaching baseball's fundamentals is important to me because I know how important they are in the overall appearance and performance of a player. There are too many people in the game today—even at the major-league level—who don't understand how to play properly. It's not that they *can't* understand, they just have to want it. A coach can teach you fundamentals until he's blue in the face, but you need to have a desire to learn and a desire to succeed before you're really going to hear his message. The same holds true for my coaching you through this book.

MY GOAL

My main goal for *Good As Gold* is to help you improve your fundamental baseball skills to become a better player or coach. This book is written for baseball players at all levels, from little leaguers to major leaguers, and for those who coach them. It is intended to give you a tool that you can use year-round to improve your skills. Becoming a good baseball player takes a lot of hard work. In order to have a long and successful baseball career, you should strive to master every area of the game. If you are a good defensive player who can't hit, you won't be as valuable to your team. If you can hit the ball, but you catch a cold easier than you can catch a ball, you won't be as valuable to your team. If you have a cannon for an arm in the outfield but you couldn't hit the cut-off man if he were 10 feet tall, you won't be as valuable to your team. If you're a fast runner but you don't know how to run the bases properly, you won't be as valuable to your team. Do you get the picture? A complete, fundamentally sound player can have a long life in baseball.

MY BEST ADVICE

"To be a complete player, you have to work at all of the fundamentals. When I went down to the batting cage, I worked on hitting the ball to right field and then up the middle and then to left. I always had a plan when I went in there. When the rest of my group was hitting, I'd run around the bases three or four times, working on my base running. In the outfield during BP, I had a coach hitting the ball off the wall so I could work on that aspect. I worked on all phases because I didn't want to be a one-dimensional player. You only get better when you continuously work at getting better."

—Amos Otis, five-time All-Star outfielder, and one of the most fundamentally sound, all-around players I've seen

I hope this book will help potential baseball players want to be complete baseball players. You don't want to be good only at hitting. You don't want to be good only at defense. You want to be an all-around player so that when you're done playing the game, you can be confident that you were the best player that you could be.

There are lots of major-league players who are good all-around players. Two who come to mind immediately are outfielder Kenny Lofton and second baseman Roberto Alomar. Players such as Lofton and Alomar know how to exploit the other team's inexperience. They know how to think at the plate. They know how to think well defensively. They know what they can do and what they cannot do. They don't try to do things on the field that they know they can't do. Those are things that make you a good player, a smart player. I will often use the word "smart" in this book, because if you're going to be a superstar, you need to think on the field. There haven't been many great players who weren't smart on the field.

THE LAYOUT

Over the next several chapters, you will be taught the fundamentals of nearly every aspect of baseball—defense, hitting, base running, throwing, conditioning plus the mental side. Again, to be a "complete" player, you must work on each of these areas.

It's important for all players to learn how to hit and how to catch. Beyond that, it's important to learn the other phases of the game and what it takes to win. That's not to say that this book is going to help you win every battle at the plate, or that you'll never make an error in the field, but by reading this book you will have a better knowledge of what to do and in what situation to do it. Learning the when-tos and when-not-tos often progresses a player's development.

Throughout my career, I've been around some of baseball's greatest players, managers, thinkers, and young stars. Since I'm not an expert at every facet of baseball, some of those great influences will share their knowledge and experience all through the book, in various quote boxes. You've already seen a couple of examples. Throughout the book, these guys will offer advice or point out the most difficult aspect of fundamental baseball for them.

Besides those quote boxes, there will be other sidebars that you'll notice. I've added "White's Words of Wisdom," which are some dos and don'ts that I recommend you follow to improve your baseball skills.

In the interest of political correctness, I want to address the usage of some words you'll frequently come across in the text. Baseball is a game that has grown in popularity for boys AND girls. And why not? If girls want to play baseball and can, they should be allowed to. However, throughout *Good As Gold* I use male genders—he, his, him, etc.—to eliminate confusion in switching back and forth. On the flip side of that, baseball is one sport that has a different term for its head coach: manager. I realize that high school and college levels oftentimes use "head coach" instead of "manager." In this book, they mean the same.

One of the most important points that I'd like you to take from this book is that baseball is like a chess match—there are basic moves, but every now and then you have to improvise through instincts.

Despite popular opinion, the game is not all about hitting. There are many teams that could improve if they only played better fundamental baseball—bunting, hitting behind runners, advancing runners, running the bases to exploit the defense, making the right decisions defensively, outfielders hitting cut-off men. There are many keys to being a championship team other than just hitting.

Until teams start developing smarter players—guys who are willing to be good all-around players—those teams are going to suffer. There's no secret to why certain teams win all the time. At the major-league level you can look at clubs that seem to be in the playoff hunt each year, like the New York Yankees and the Atlanta Braves. They're in a great position every year largely because they play fundamentally sound baseball.

Baseball is a sport that can be enjoyed by everyone. Simply put, the game is fun. In a story you'll see detailed later in the book, my dad told me, "If you're going to play this game, then you have to learn how to enjoy this game. The only way you learn how to enjoy this game is to play the game."

Good As Gold might not answer every question you have about playing baseball (although it'll come close), but it certainly will teach you how to play fundamentally. When you know how to become a fundamentally sound player, you'll become a better player, you'll help your team become better, and you will make this great game even more enjoyable for yourself, your teammates, coaches, and even the spectators.

So, grab your gear and let's go...

Chapter 2

Gold Glove Defense

For a team that expects to win, I look at defense as being the most important asset that it can have. Many people out there would put pitching first and defense second, but I put defense first because good defense can help mediocre pitching. If you have great pitching and no defense, then that pitching is not going to flourish.

Some managers and coaches want to place all of their emphasis on offense. While that can make sense on the surface, those teams are often going to lose games with scores like 11-9 or 9-8. They have a slugfest every night. Whichever team succumbs to the bombardment is the team that is going to lose.

At the college level, coaches try to put together more of a defensive team first, and then put pitching with it. The major-league mentality says pitching first, then offense, and finally defense. When you get into the last couple of weeks of the season, when everything is on the line, everyone first cries for defense and pitching.

You want to put your best defensive team on the field and then put pitching with that and hope that you can win a game with a score of 2-1 or 3-2. If two equally matched pitchers are on the mound, chances are it's going to be a low-scoring game. The difference in that game is going to be defense and what a fielder did or didn't do, on a move the manager did or didn't make.

THE "BASICS" OF A DEFENSIVE PLAYER

Defense can be taught enough to make players adequate, but one thing that can't be taught is "soft hands." "Soft hands" means a player has the ability to catch the ball smoothly and transfer it smoothly from one hand to the other to make a throw. For instance, if the ball keeps popping out of the catcher's mitt, it means he doesn't have soft hands. The same thing happens to other infielders. If the ball keeps popping out of their gloves, then they have hard

MY TOUGHEST FUNDAMENTAL

"Developmentally, for me and a lot of other shortstops, it was difficult understanding the rhythm and the timing of the throw to first base. During my first year of rookie ball, I made 32 errors in 60 games. Most of them were throwing errors. Things were easier once I understood the timing and made accurate throws."

———*Cal Ripken Jr., one of the most consistent shortstops I've ever seen*

Photo by Matt Fulks

hands. Soft hands are directly related to a player's feet, his positioning, and his hand-eye coordination, because he has to have the ability to read the ball and be in a good fielding position to make the play.

All good defensive players have command of hand-eye coordination. They have quick feet, which is a must because the quicker the feet, the quicker a player can throw and cover ground. That is especially important when you are talking about first-step quickness and going left or right. Solid defensive players should possess good throwing mechanics. Good defense is not only catching the ball, but also knowing when to throw the ball.

When trying to find good defensive players in the infield, coaches should look for positioning when players field ground balls, how their feet are set, and how they come through the ball. In the outfield, coaches should see how players get behind the fly ball and come through the ball if the runner is tagging up.

A good defensive player wants the ball hit to him on every play. That shows that he is a very confident player and that he feels he can make the play, and he *wants* to make the play. As soon as the ball is hit, and based on how the ball is hit, he reacts to it instinctively. That good defensive player realizes the importance of knowing what he's going to do with the ball before it's hit to him.

MY BEST ADVICE

"Always anticipate the ball being hit to you. When it is hit to you on the ground, stay down and keep your hands out in front of your body."
—*Roberto Alomar, Gold Glove second baseman*

A common mistake that defensive players make is that if they are offensive minded, they may have had a bad trip to the plate, or they may have been robbed on a hit, and in turn, they take their offense out to the field. Rather than thinking about playing defense, they are still thinking about that out they made or that great play that someone made on a ball that they hit hard. That forces them to lose defensive concentration, making them more apt to make mistakes.

Good defensive players have to study hitters. They have to know each hitter's strength and play to that strength. If the hitter does something totally different, then we can't do anything about that. But it is important that defensive players know the hitter and the situation.

Communication is another key to playing defense. On pop ups or on fly balls where two guys come together, we try to get our players to yell, "I got it!" three times to make sure that someone hears. Outfielders catch more balls through communication and positioning. They have signs that they give each other to say, "I'm going to take the short one, you take the long one," or vice versa, so outfielders are not running into each other. For instance, the center fielder might give the right fielder a sign that says, "OK, you're playing deeper than me, so if the ball is hit short, I'm going to go first, and you back me up."

There are some important elements to consider when thinking about defensive play, regardless of the player's position in the field. The first thing to do is determine what type of player he is. That will give you some indication of how well he can play defense at a certain position. You should look at his pre-pitch stance and his ready stance. You need to look at how he reacts when a ball is hit to him, and how he positions himself to catch it. Those are all skills that good defensive players possess.

TAKE PRIDE

Defensive play is mainly what got me to the major leagues. I knew that if I were going to stay in the major leagues for any length of time, it was going to be because of my ability to play defense, including my ability to make good decisions at the right time. You should work to be one of those players who is able to see the play before it happens, and factor in all the possibilities before the pitch is made.

Baseball doesn't have a playbook or a clock, so nothing happens until the ball is actually hit. That allows the defensive player time to plot various scenarios. If you have a man on first, for instance, think to yourself, "OK, if the ball is hit to me, what am I going to do with it? If it's hit hard, what am I going to do? If it's hit soft, what am I going to do? If it's hit to my left or right, how will I play it?" Each possibility needs to be factored. When the pitch is made, your mind goes blank, concentrating on that ball to the plate. Then when the ball is hit, you can react immediately to the play and know your responsibility without having to waste that split second to decide what you're going to do. You have to react to what you see, but what you see is something that has already been preprogrammed in your mind.

Pride in your defense, not only individually but also as a team, is critical to reach true success. The attitude in baseball is that defense makes good pitching. Good players make the routine plays routinely because they practice good, consistent work habits. Consistent defense, day in and day out, comes from preparing and knowing what everyone does on every play.

You must have dedication to be a good defensive player. You need that desire and pride that says, "I want to be better than you." When I played, I wanted to be better than Willie Randolph for that three-game series against the New York Yankees. I wanted to be better than Detroit's Lou Whitaker for that three-game series, or whomever was playing my position for the other team in that particular series. I think that's why I became who I was as a player.

General fielding

TOOLS OF THE TRADE

Different positions use different types and sizes of fielding gloves. Usually, outfielders have bigger gloves than infielders, while catchers and first basemen use completely different mitts. When I played second base, I chose a smaller glove because I felt the most important thing I had to do at second was to turn the double play. With a smaller glove, I could quickly take the ball out without "losing" it.

Parents often buy their kids the biggest gloves they can find, hoping their son or daughter will grow into it. That's really not the proper way to buy a glove, even for a little league player. We always need to buy a glove that fits our hand. Keep in mind that when catching a baseball, you catch it with your fingers, not with the palm of your hand. So if the glove doesn't fit properly, it can actually hurt your defensive ability.

RESTING AND READY STANCES

Defensive players have two basic stances, resting and ready. The resting stance is when nothing is happening, usually while the pitcher is getting the signs from the catcher, or the manager has made a pitching change. Use the resting stance, which is simply placing both hands on your knees, when no action is happening on the field.

When the pitcher has his sign and is ready to make the pitch, you get in the ready stance. In the ready stance, you bend at the knees with your hands out front, your head up, looking for the pitch. Remember, when you're watching the ball to the plate, you're not watching the ball out of the pitcher's hand. You should pick an area in front of the plate, before the ball goes into the hitting zone, and concentrate on that particular area.

You should see the pitcher in your peripheral vision. When he starts winding up, you start positioning yourself so that when the ball enters the hitting area in front of home plate—when it goes from grass to dirt—you're in your ready stance. If you watch the ball out of the pitcher's hand, then your timing is not going to allow you to be able to react quickly to a ball that comes off the bat at a high rate of speed.

A good, general resting stance.

Anticipate the ball being hit to you in your ready stance.

"GET DOWN ON IT"

The stance that I used to field groundballs was feet shoulder-width apart, bent at the knees rather than at the waist, and on the balls of my feet. (When you bend at the waist, your knees will lock, and it's difficult to get down low enough to properly field a ground ball.) You want your rear end down, with your hands out in front of your body. As the ball is approaching, I prefer having the throwing hand over the glove to help avoid the ball easily hopping out. (With your throwing hand to the side, a ground ball can roll out of your glove and up your arm.) Your lower body should be pointing in a straight line toward the ball. You don't want your feet pointing out or in.

As the ball is moving closer, your feet are a little wider than shoulder-width apart until you see the ball take a hop that you want to catch. Keep your feet moving until you see your hop. When you see the ball take the hop that you want, widen your base at the point of fielding the ball, take a crow hop, and then

Figure 2-3

release the throw. I feel that if you're a right-handed fielder, regardless of your position on the infield, your left foot should be slightly ahead of your right when fielding (Figure 2-3).

Once the ball is at your glove, you should try to field "through" it, which allows you to get into a crow hop a little faster and lets your legs help you make the long throw across the field. If you get back on your heels, get flat-footed or stop your body at the point of fielding a ball, you have to start all over and use your man-made energy, which puts most of the pressure on your throwing shoulder.

I don't like the one-knee approach because you lose your mobility and you can't react quickly if the ball gets away from you.

Some coaches teach players to get down on one knee to field a grounder. I don't prefer that approach, because once you're down on one knee, all mobility is lost. If you're down on one knee and the ball takes a bad hop, you're more susceptible to injury. Another reason I don't like the one-knee approach is that if the ball does take a bad hop and bounces off you, you have to pick up your entire body and run after the ball. If you stay on your feet, balanced on the balls of your feet, and the grounder takes a bad hop, you can go in any direction in an attempt to keep it in front of you.

PLAYING THE POP-UP OR FLY BALL

Even though different positions have different ways of playing a ball in the air, there are certain principles that hold true for every position. One of the biggest mistakes made when trying to catch a pop-up is that as the ball leaves the bat, players often run to where the ball is going up.

Unfortunately, the ball almost always comes down at a different angle than it goes up. When a ball is popped up on the first base side of the infield, for example, it doesn't come straight down; it comes back toward the infield. When a ball is going up, the fielder should start to position himself so that when the ball reaches its highest point, he's able to anticipate the direction it will travel downward.

Once you're under the pop-up and you feel secure about where it's going to come down, you need to get ready to make the catch. As the ball is coming down, flex

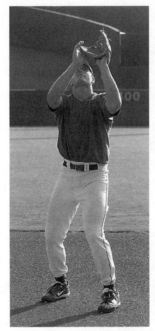

When catching a pop-up or fly, you should flex your knees, have your glove up and try to catch with two hands.

your knees a little so you're able to cradle the ball. Don't shield it from your face with the glove. You need to see the ball to catch it. Keep your glove to the throwing-arm side of your face, above your head, and whenever possible, use two hands to catch the ball.

Using two hands isn't always possible, and some "older" players prefer to use one because that's how they learned to play growing up. At the major-league level, I have worked with several "life-long" one-handed catching outfielders. We basically have to let them continue playing that way until something tells him or the coach that he needs to make a change.

Some guys are better at catching one-handed. Amos Otis, with whom I played for 11 years with the Royals, was a one-handed fielder who was very good at transferring the ball to his right hand, his throwing hand. Amos also happened to win three Gold Glove awards during his career.

MY BEST ADVICE

"When I was first learning the game, my brothers tried to teach me to catch with two hands, which I did. Then I had a teammate in 1970 with the Royals named Pat Kelly, who had trouble catching fly balls. He had both hands in the air waiting for the ball. I told him how all sorts of things can happen when both hands are in the air too long. To show him what I was talking about, I wouldn't raise my throwing hand to catch the ball. Catching with one hand started to feel so good that it was natural. I stayed with it. I had a rhythm that allowed me to get rid of the ball on my throws a lot quicker after I caught it. But I wouldn't teach kids to try that. It has to come naturally."
—*Amos Otis, member of the Royals' first Hall of Fame class in 1986*

So catching with two hands is not something that every player *must* do in order to succeed. However, I think at a teaching level early in a player's career, he should learn how to use two hands in catching fly balls and ground balls. When players get to the major-league level, it depends on the skill level of the player if he can be good at it or if he needs to make a change to two hands.

Even though players always should try to use two hands when catching a fly ball, it's most important when a runner is tagging up. Oftentimes, if two hands aren't up there ready to step through the ball to make the transfer and get that throw off, the runner will take advantage of the defensive player. Catching the ball with one hand will put the fielder in an awkward position, because after making the catch, he has to bring the ball to the other hand, forcing him to take too many steps before he gets rid of the ball. Good base runners will take advantage of that situation, and likely reach the next base.

In terms of priorities on pop-ups or fly balls, the shortstop has priority over the second baseman and the third baseman. The second baseman has priority over the first baseman. The corner guys—first base and third base— have priority over the catcher as long as they make that call early enough. Usually, everyone in the infield has priority over the pitcher. In the outfield, the center fielder has priority over the left and right fielders. Generally, the out-fielders have priority over the infielders on balls that are in shallow outfield, because they are charging toward the action.

If the infielder squares up his back to the outfield, the outfielder knows that the infielder is going to catch the ball. As long as the infielder runs side-ways toward the ball, then the outfielder has the right to call off the infielder. Only in the case of a runner being on third base in a tag-up situation does the outfielder have complete priority to come in and run the infielder off the ball, because the outfielder is going toward the plate and the infielder is going away from the plate. The outfielder has a better opportunity to hold the runner at third. If there is a fly ball to medium outfield and there is a guy tagging up on third, normally the infielder would be yelling, "Tag! Tag! Tag!" because the outfielder would be looking up toward the ball. That verbal call tells the out-fielder that he has to catch the ball and throw it home.

Since multiple players could be going for the same ball, communication is extremely important. The most commonly used (and effective) phrase in baseball by the outfielders and infielders is yelling, "I got it! I got it! I got it!" You can't be bashful when yelling for the ball. The off player, the one who is being called off, should say either, "You take it," or simply, "Take it." That helps you relax and know that it's your play, without having to be concerned about any type of collision with another fielder.

WHICH STEP DO YOU CHOOSE?

There are two main moves to use on the fly ball if you have to run a long way for the ball: the drop step and the diagonal step. The drop step, which is used mainly by an outfielder, is a move you make to go back on a ball, or to cut a ball off in the alley (Figure 2-6). If the ball is hit directly over your head, from your ready posi-tion you step directly back with either your right foot or left foot, crossover with your trailing foot, keeping your eye on the ball whenever possible. That move will help you get

Figure 2-6

Figure 2-7   Figure 2-8   Figure 2-9

to the ball faster than first back-pedaling or running at an angle. The key is to get back as fast as you can.

The diagonal step, which also is known as the cross-over, is a direct move to your right or left to cut a ball off, whether the ball is a line drive, pop fly or on the ground (Figures 2-7, 2-8 and 2-9).

If the ball is hit into the alley, you're going to use a drop step to hit the right angle that will take you to the point where you want to meet the ball. Depending on how hard the ball is hit, you will use a diagonal step to meet it straight across, the drop step to meet the ball at a point if it is hit harder toward the gap, or the drop step if the ball is hit over your head.

It takes a lot of practice and experience to know the best way to reach a ball. This is an area of the game where your depth perception and your hearing ability come in to play—the ability to read and hear a ball off the bat. At a younger age, it is more difficult to "hear" how hard a ball is hit because of the aluminum bats. When a ball is hit with an aluminum bat, all you get is a little "ping" sound, and it's tough to tell how hard the ball has been hit, and some-times it will cause the player to get a bad jump on the ball. With a wood bat, you can pretty much tell how hard a ball has been hit just by the sound it makes.

LET'S GO TO THE HOP

Already in this chapter, you have come across the term "crow hop," which may be a new term for you. The crow hop is a move used by infielders and outfielders to gain balance and momentum before making a throw. Crow hops are used on all throws.

To execute the crow hop, as you field the ball and come through it, raise your left leg (if you're a right-handed thrower) take one to two short hops on your right leg, and then throw the ball. If you throw left-handed, you will raise your right leg and hop on your left. Be sure to let your legs work for you to give you a stronger throw and to keep extra strain off your shoulder. As you can tell, this is the way to get your balance (raised leg), momentum (the hops) and power (planting after the last hop).

After you field a grounder, thrust up with your glove-side leg, take one or two short hops and release a strong throw.

Most of the time your hop is going to be short if you're an infielder, unless, for example, you're a third baseman making a long throw from the line over to first. In fact, infielders sometimes look more like they're taking a shuffle instead of an actual hop. The hop will be longer if you're an outfielder. In general, the farther your throw, the longer your crow hop is going to be. The more power you have to generate, the longer that step needs to be.

However, don't feel restricted to always taking only one or two steps before you release the ball. There might be times for a second baseman or a pitcher, when a ground ball is hit so sharply to you that the first baseman isn't at the bag when you're ready to throw. In that instance, you might have to make one or two more crow hops before the first baseman is set to receive your throw.

There may also be times when you don't have the proper throwing grip on the baseball after you finish your first crow hop. Just keep going through the crow hop until you have the grip that you need for the throw (see chapter 5 for the proper way to grip a baseball).

On either of those plays, if your body were to stop instead of continuing the crow hop, then you're dead in the water because you've lost all momentum and oomph behind your throw. Remember, though, the crow hop's main purpose is balance and rhythm to help you make a strong, accurate throw to the proper place.

BATTLING THE SUN AND THE "HIGH" SKY

One of the toughest jobs for any defensive player is battling the sun. When playing a ball in the sun, keep in mind that if the ball is in the direct center of the sun, you're not likely to catch it. You're not going to see it whether you have dark sunglasses or not. For a ball in the sun, always try to keep the ball on the edge of the sun by angling your body and utilizing your throwing hand to help shield the sun from your eyes. You can use your glove to shield the sun away from the ball, but remember not to blind yourself from the ball.

In addition to the sun, a lot of times fielders have to play against what we call a "high" sky. With a high sky, you're not necessarily dealing with the sun, but you're dealing with a really bright sky. The only way to battle a high sky is with dark glasses, the best being the flip-downs. Even then the high sky can be very difficult, but using sunglasses is the only way to battle it.

GOTCHA!

A fun game that I used to play growing up was what we called "hot box" or "pickle" (technically called a rundown), where you and another guy have a runner trapped between bases. When you have someone caught in a rundown, you want to close the distance between you and the runner, and you want him going back to the base from where he came. Ideally, you want the runner going full speed in the opposite direction before you release the ball. When you have the ball, make sure that the receiver is on the same side as your throwing arm, and avoid faking throws. Have a consistent arm position, holding the ball in sight, then when the receiver yells, "Now!" release the ball so he can tag the runner (Figure 2-13). The receiver may also take one step forward to indicate that he is ready for the ball. Remember to reduce the number of throws.

If you're a pitcher who has caught the runner too far off base between first and second, or second and third, try not to run directly toward the runner. Pitchers aren't used to being in that situation, so the quick runner can

Figure 2-13

oftentimes fake out a pitcher who is coming straight at him. As a pitcher in that situation, you should run at an angle to get behind the runner and make him head back toward his original base. That way, whatever moves the runner makes won't fake you out.

BEFORE WE GET STARTED

Those are the general rules that should be followed by all defensive players to become fundamentally sound. Of course, there are special plays and rules for each position on the field and ways to effectively play a certain spot. The highlights of the individualized positions are next.

First base

Mark McGwire

Unfortunately in baseball there are two positions that people believe anyone can play: first base and left field. If a guy can hit, managers feel that they can hide those guys at first or in left if he doesn't fit well at any other position. However, you really can't hide anyone in baseball. It's unfortunate that certain positions in the game are given less credit as being important. I just don't think the game was designed for that thinking. Every position on the field is important for a team's success.

The first baseman is like an anchor. He has to be there to steady the ship because he handles the ball more than anyone else on the field besides the pitcher and catcher. He takes all the throws from the infielders, some throws from the catcher, and throws from the pitcher on pick-off attempts. So he's actually handling the ball more than anyone on the field when everything is totaled at the end of the season.

The first baseman should be a guy with some agility; a guy who can maneuver his feet on errant throws and can position himself to make the tough plays in the dirt. He needs to be smart enough to know when to come off the bag to make a close play look good enough that the umpire might give them the out. The first baseman has a strong role in being able to field his position. He has to know how far right he can go in the hole between first and second. It really helps if he's the guy who can catch pop ups not only over his head, but also down the right field line. He has to be able to come in and field bunts and read situations on a bunt. One of the most difficult plays for a first baseman is to field a ground ball hit to him with a man on first, make the throw to second and get back to first for a possible double play. The first baseman also should know when to leave the bag on bad throws to keep the ball from getting by him.

A good first baseman needs soft hands. When I played with John Mayberry, he was a guy who basically said that no matter how you have to throw the ball, just make sure it's low. He was one of the "old school" guys who used to stretch way out there. He had soft hands. Some of the other "old school" guys, like George Scott, were mobile, could play their position, and pick balls out of the dirt. Mark McGwire didn't have a lot of range left and right, but he was able to pick the ball out of the dirt. He was a true first baseman. Many guys who play first aren't true first basemen.

For the infielders, the ability of a first baseman helps give them a lot of confidence. Infielders know that they can make a quick play, and if they get the throw off in that direction, the first baseman can catch balls three feet inside the bag or scoop the ball out of the dirt. That gets the out and saves the other infielder an error. Believe me, that's a great feeling for the infielders.

BEING READY

One of the important keys for a first baseman is his pre-pitch stance. When we see a first baseman who appears to have a problem with range left or right, oftentimes it goes back to his pre-pitch stance. The first baseman needs to be ready when the ball is in the hitting zone, with his knees bent, with his weight on the balls of his feet, hands out in front. He's ready to go left or right, being able to cover the bag on any type of throw from any of the infielders.

We don't encourage the first baseman to play on the line unless a left-handed batter is a strong pull hitter. Usually the first baseman is five to seven feet off the line, probably 10-12 feet behind the bag at first, in what we call a straight-up position. Closer to the line is a pull position. We want to protect that area between first and second as much as we can, because more balls are going to be hit through that hole than down the line.

On a ground ball, the first baseman's biggest responsibility is to get to the bag. He has to be able to position himself so that if there is a throw in the dirt, he can maneuver his feet enough to get into position to scoop that ball out. He has to always expect a bad throw from the infield and adjust down the line so he can catch the ball and tag the runner.

The first baseman shouldn't keep infielders waiting to make their throw. The infielders don't like to catch a ball and then have to wait for the first baseman to get to the bag. As soon as that ball is hit, the first baseman has to be on that bag so the infielders can get to the ball and get rid of it as soon as they can.

When waiting for a throw from another infielder, the first baseman should extend out and give the fielder a good target, being careful not to stretch too soon.

DRILLS

First basemen need to go through drills to work on the high throws, throws down the baseline, throws in the dirt, holding runners on first, pick-off attempts from the pitcher, tagging on a pick-off attempt from the catcher, and breaking off the bag into a fielding position when they're holding the runner at first and the pitch is made.

They have to know how far to come off to protect their position so the ball won't be hit past them. They have to know how to play behind the runner at first base and still hold him close to try to keep him from stealing the base.

First basemen need to work on their communication with the pitcher. They need to work on the 3-6-3 double play, which is when there is a runner on first base and the ball is grounded to the first baseman, he throws the ball to the shortstop covering second and then comes back to the base to cover on the return throw.

He needs to work on the cutoff position when receiving throws from the outfield on a ball to right field. He needs to learn what kind of arm the outfielder has so he'll know how deep he needs to be in order to make a good throw to home plate. The first baseman needs to know that on a pop fly, the second baseman has priority over him unless he's in foul territory or over by the fence. The only play a first baseman can't work on is diving for balls. Luckily or not, most of that is instinctive.

DEFENDING THE SAC

For a "typical" sacrifice situation with the guy on base, first the pitcher has to throw a strike and try to make the hitter bunt. Once the bunt is down, if the first baseman sees the ball going toward third base, he should get back to the bag and not go running down the line just to run down there. Much depends on the type of play that your team is running. Some teams run the play where the first baseman breaks early and tries to be close to home to field the bunt quickly to get the runner at second. Either way, the first baseman's primary responsibility is to make sure he gets one out.

If you know the offense is trying a sacrifice, the pitcher should throw a strike, the second baseman covers first, and the first and third basemen come down the line. If the first baseman gets the ball, the key is that he at least gets the out at first base. Each team has some trick play to try to get the runner out. I don't really encourage high school or college coaches to have the second baseman cover first at the last possible moment on bunt plays. I always felt that was a dangerous play because the second baseman is running hard to get to the bag, and the runner is charging hard to be safe. Players have been injured trying to make that play. The right way to run that play is for the second baseman to go to first base, and the first baseman to try to go down the line to field the ball. If the ball is bunted to third, the second baseman falls back at that time and the first baseman covers the bag.

When I was playing second base, I would always tell my first baseman that anytime a right-handed hitter pushed the ball between the pitcher and first base, or a left hander dragged between the pitcher toward second base, to let me take everything that was not down the line. If the ball is down the line, then the first baseman should go for it, because when a hitter bunts in a non-sacrifice situation, chances are he is a fast runner and most of those guys can beat the pitcher to first base. In those situations, I let the first baseman know that I would be at first waiting for his throw.

HOLDING RUNNERS

When the first baseman is holding a runner on base, his right foot should be on the inside of the bag—not straddling the bag—and his body should be angled so that he can be squared to the pitcher. He wants to be in position so that

Figure 2-16

when the pitcher throws over to first, he can make as quick a tag as possible to try to get the runner out (Figures 2-16 and 2-17).

Figure 2-17

CUT! CUT! CUT!

The first baseman's initial responsibility before taking a cut-off throw from the center fielder or right fielder is to know the arm strength of that outfielder. Once the ball is hit, he lines himself up between the catcher and the right fielder so that the right fielder has a target. He wants to position himself in a spot on the field so that the right fielder is throwing the ball "through" him. Ideally, the ball should come in about head high. By throwing the ball through him, if the first baseman were to let the ball pass, it should be able to take one hop and be in the catcher's mitt. If the first baseman is "too high"—too close to home plate—then the right fielder is likely to throw the ball over his head and over the catcher's head. The first baseman has to know the depth that he is going to need in order for the right fielder to make a one-hop throw to the catcher.

COMMON MISTAKES

A common mistake regarding first base is that coaches tend to think that they can put anyone in that position. That is not a good philosophy because first basemen do handle the ball a great deal of the time, especially in crucial situations.

A common mistake that first basemen make is that a lot of them are not able to catch pop ups because their approach is wrong. First basemen are often taught that on a pop up toward the stands, they should go toward the stands and then work their way from there, even though pop ups that go up on the right field side almost always come back down toward the infield. We still see first basemen run to the fence, and then have to back pedal rapidly to adjust to the ball, which makes them end up falling over backward. First basemen need to learn how to let the ball get as high as it is going to get and then gradually position themselves under the ball as it comes down.

Second base

A coach should really be ecstatic if he gets a second baseman who has a lot of range and turns a very good double play. One of the most difficult aspects about playing second base is turning a double play because you don't see the runner until the last minute. As a shortstop you see the runner the whole way because everything is in front of you, but the second baseman doesn't have that luxury.

A tough part of the job for second base is most of the time you are playing with your back to first. Plus the grounder up the middle, where the second baseman has to get the ball back to first, is just as difficult as the shortstop going into the hole toward third and having to make a long throw to first. However, the double play definitely is the most difficult thing about playing second base.

TURNING TWO...EASY AS 1-2-3

The double play is just like a ballet at second base. It's almost like going to the Arthur Murray Dance Studio and doing your 1-2-3. There are three steps to a double play. You tag the bag with your left foot...that's one. You catch the ball on your next step, which is your right foot...that's two. Then you throw to first base on your next step...that's three.

You just have to make a determination of how fast or slow you have to execute it based on how hard the ball is hit. The toughest thing for a second baseman turning a double play is that his head is pointed toward third base, meaning that he sees the runner coming toward him for the first time once he receives the ball and he's ready for the third step. So if the runner is all over him, he has to make a lot of quick decisions in a short period of time, such as if he should throw the ball or hold it, and if he throws the ball how he's going to escape the runner.

If the second baseman decides that he's going to throw the ball and jump over the runner, he actually must throw the ball before he jumps up. His athletic ability is going to determine how well he can make that play. If he doesn't have quick feet, it's hard to turn a double play, especially on that play. The quicker he sets his feet, the quicker his arm speed goes. Then with a runner on top of him, he has to be able to get up off the ground. If he gets hit after he's in the air, it's hard to get hurt. The second baseman just doesn't want to get caught with his spikes in the ground when he gets hit.

Frank White

I didn't get spiked by a lot by runners coming into second, but I got kicked frequently, so I bought a soccer shin guard and wore it under my socks. I didn't get spiked much because I had a matador way of jumping around the runner. The reason many second basemen have trouble with an oncoming runner is that they try to jump over the runner. I learned from Cookie Rojas, my predecessor with the Royals, that you should jump around the runner, like a bull going under a bullfighter's cape. One advantage of going around the runner is that usually the leg that a runner hits is the leg that is going up. So if you're jumping around the runner and that leg gets hit, then you spin around without a lot of physical damage being done.

For a second baseman, there are three approaches to deal with when turning the double play at second base from a ground ball—the ball straight at you, the ball to your left, or the ball to your right.

When the ball is coming directly to you, position yourself to receive it in front, with both hands down, bent at the knees, with your weight on the balls of your feet, and your upper body aimed straight toward the ball. As the ball is about to enter your glove, drop your right foot back, which opens up your hips toward the second base bag, giving you a clear throw to the shortstop covering. Remember that if you don't open your hips, your feet will have to come off the ground physically to pivot and make the throw. Obviously that will take away timing that is precious to turning the double play.

When a runner is on first and a grounder is coming directly at the second baseman, he should open his hips and make a quick toss to the shortstop covering second base.

When the ball is slightly to your left, you should shuffle your feet to get in front of it. You always want to stay in front of the ball whenever possible. Once you're in line to receive it, use the same approach that you did when the ball was straight at you. Whenever possible, keep your feet on the ground to help make the play quicker.

If the ball is too far to your left, where you really have to reach for it, and there's no hope of getting in front of it, then use the cross-over step or jab step. Hustle to the ball, secure it off your left foot, and let the momentum spin you around to make a true overhand throw to second base.

The problem you can run into with a ball to your extreme left that you can't get to is that you end up fielding it in front of your left foot, then you have to fight your body's momentum to turn around and make a throw. Oftentimes, because of your body's momentum on that play, you have to make a side-arm throw, which tails away from the shortstop covering second. Remember, on this play that your main objective is to get the runner out at second; if a double play is turned, then it's a bonus.

If the ball is not to your extreme right, shuffle over to get in front of it, and then make an underhanded toss to the shortstop, hitting him chest high.

When you make an underhanded toss, keep the ball in plain view for the shortstop. That will help him concentrate on it as much as possible. The reason for the chest-high toss is that it makes it easier for him to handle. Shortstops are usually charging toward the bag quickly, so you want to make things as simple as possible.

If the groundball is to your extreme right, you have to immediately deter-mine if you will throw an underhanded shuffle pass to the shortstop, or if you're going to try to beat the runner to the bag yourself.

If the grounder is too far to your left that you can't get in front of it, you'll need to spin and make a good throw to second.

You need to make a cross-over step (left foot first) to go for the ball, then decide which play you're going to make. If you decide to take the ball yourself, always be sure to yell, "I got it!" That will help the shortstop know that he needs to get out of the way. When you take the play yourself, most times you're going to hit the bag with your right foot, and then try to make the throw to first.

When playing second base, in one of the field's double-play positions, there are a few rules of thumb you need to keep in mind. First, know the running speed of the hitter and of the runner on first base. If the ball is hit to your left and the runner going to second has already passed you when you get the ball, that will help you determine if you should throw to second to get him or just throw to first to get the hitter. If the ball is hit directly at you or just a

If you can shuffle over to a grounder hit to your right, you can make an underhand toss to the shortstop.

little to your left, the rule of thumb that I used was that if the runner had already passed my right shoulder, then I would throw to first. If the runner hadn't passed me by the time I received the ball, then I would throw to second for the possible double play.

As you get older and start playing more as a second baseman, be careful in a double-play situation when you want to tag the runner on his way to second base. If you decide to secure the ball planning to tag the runner in the baseline, remember that he does not have to slide at that point. So be prepared for the runner to do something out of the ordinary—he might try to run into you or cross-body block you. Always be familiar with that runner at first base to help you determine if you're going to take the conventional double-play approach, or if you're going to attempt to tag the runner and then throw to first. Oftentimes the situation of the game at that particular point will help dictate which route you choose.

MY TOUGHEST FUNDAMENTAL

"Learning how to turn the double play—footwork around the bag, learning to protect myself, and still get a good, strong throw over to first base."
—*Roberto Alomar, Gold Glove second baseman*

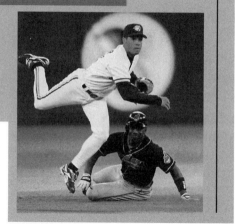

COMMON MISTAKES

One of the most common errors I see from young second basemen is if there is a runner stealing second base, and the hitter hits the ball, the second baseman vacates his area too soon and allows the ball to get through for a base hit, creating a first-and-third situation. Another common mistake is when a second baseman goes to turn the double play, he often doesn't see the ball into the glove. Instead, he feels that runner coming and he wants to take a quick peak to see where that guy is before seeing the ball. Usually, the ball drops and he doesn't get either out. Another common mistake is not knowing what type of evasive move to make on certain double plays based on the situation and the runner.

WHITE'S WORDS OF WISDOM

• Don't peak on double plays. Stay with the ball until it's in your glove.
• Don't stand flat-footed on second base after you throw the ball to first base on double plays. Make sure you get up in the air so you won't get hurt.
• Always make sure you catch the ball before starting your throw.
• If you don't field the grounder cleanly, you should always understand at second base that you still have an opportunity to throw a runner out at first because you have a short throw.
• Always communicate with your first baseman. Let him know how far away you're playing and always let him know what balls to go for and what balls not to go for.

Second base/Shortstop

The middle infield is the only position on the field that can't be run from the bench. The second baseman and shortstop have to make all their decisions based on what they know and the situation on the field at the time. There are several instances where it is imperative that the second baseman and shortstop work together on the field. This is especially true when there is at least one runner on base. There also are several situations that apply to only those two positions.

One of the responsibilities between the second baseman and the shortstop when there is a runner on first base is to decide who's going to cover the bag on a ball hit back to the pitcher. If the second baseman is going to cover the base, he needs to get to the bag and with his glove up, be ready to receive the throw. The speed of the runner from first and how quickly the pitcher gets the ball to the second baseman will determine his foot placement around the base.

With a fast runner, the second baseman should put his left foot on the middle of the bag to receive the throw, then push him to the inside part of the infield to clear the runner (Figure 2-22). If the pitcher hesitates throwing the ball to second, giving the runner more time to make it a close play, the second baseman also should place his left foot on the middle of the base and be ready to make the play. With a slow runner, he can put the base between his feet and make the play from that position, with his right foot touching the bag.

Figure 2-22

A second baseman's left foot is always his tag foot, which is his first step; his second step is his catch step; and the third step is his throw step. He should make sure that he doesn't go off the back part of the bag to make the play. He should either go to the inside of the infield, or straddle the bag and go toward first base. Then once he catches the ball, he turns and throws to first.

If the shortstop is going to cover second base on the play when the ball is hit back to the pitcher, he should come to the bag and position himself so that he can catch the ball coming across the base and touch the backside corner of the base with his right foot (Figure 2-23). If there are any delays by the pitcher, the shortstop will come to the base, place his left foot on the back part of the bag, and be prepared to make the play.

Another time where it is important that the second baseman and shortstop work together is when a runner might attempt to steal second base. Whoever is taking the throw from the catcher usually rounds the back of the base and puts the base between his feet. A common error that a lot of middle infielders make is that they reach out to catch the ball, and then make a sweep tag for the runner. If the catcher has a strong arm, it is preferable to let the ball continue to travel to the center of the body, tag down on the top of the ankle of the runner, and then clear out so the runner can

Figure 2-23

slide through the bag. If you know ahead of time that a runner likes to slide with his cleats (spikes) up, you want to set up on the inside of the bag—the pitcher's mound side—instead of straddling it. This is also a good approach to take if your catcher does not have a strong arm.

SWITCHING ROLES

On balls hit to the outfield, the shortstop and second baseman have similar duties. The main concern is making sure the outfielder throws the ball to the right base. If the ball is hit to left center or to the left-field corner, for instance, the shortstop goes out first and the second baseman trails him. The

second baseman's job is to line up the shortstop with third base if there's nobody on base. If there is a fast runner on first and the ball is hit down the line or in the gap, the second baseman's lining up the shortstop to third. If the runner on first is slow, he's lining up to home.

If the ball is hit to right-center or down the right-field line then they switch roles, making it the shortstop's responsibility to trail the second baseman, lining him up to whichever base he's going to have to make the play. Usually he trails

When the second baseman and shortstop are lining up for a cutoff from the outfield, the first one gives the outfielder a target by holding up his hands, and the trailer is there to line up the first one.

about 15 feet behind him so if the ball is thrown low from the outfielder, he can yell, "Let it go!" then move up and get the ball on one hop. If it's high, then he can have the second baseman let it go, and run up to catch it in the air and make the throw to the base where it needs to be thrown.

PLAYING THE POPS

The most difficult aspect on fly balls for middle infielders is determining how deep you go into the outfield to catch it. We tell our infielders that only the outfielders use verbal signs, such as yelling, "I got it!" Since outfielders are charging toward the infield, they can see the ball easier. They can run, look up and look down, and decide if they can get to it. We tell our infielders to go back on pop flies until they hear the outfielder call for the ball.

Shortstop

A shortstop needs a lot of the same qualifications as a second baseman. He needs to have speed, range, agility, a strong arm, and the ability to think and run the game. Generally, the shortstop is one of the best athletes on the field, but he also needs to be able to make the routine play.

When thinking about the great shortstops, Cal Ripken Jr. was probably the most consistent one I had an opportunity to play against other than Mark Belanger, who was an eight-time Gold Glove winner with Baltimore. Cal was not the quickest or the fastest shortstop but he had a knack of knowing how to play hitters. He seemingly had a magnet in his glove, as he was able to make all the routine plays and occasionally make the great ones.

Then there was Ozzie Smith, whose Gold Glove career speaks for itself with his 2002 induction into the Hall of Fame. In my opinion, he's the greatest defensive player and the most athletic person ever to play shortstop.

Cal Ripken

AP/WWP

MY TOUGHEST FUNDAMENTAL

"The toughest play for anybody is the play that takes them away from the base that they're going to throw to. Besides that, I always concentrated on the routine plays. The plays that should be the easiest often become the toughest ones. You make more mistakes on the routine plays than the tough ones. The tough plays are reactionary. On the routine plays, you have too much time to think. So, you have to concentrate more."
—*Ozzie Smith, Hall of Fame shortstop*

Part of the shortstop's job is to know how to defend the hitters. He has an advantage over the second baseman when turning the double play. He needs to be able to read the situation and the batter at the plate for positioning. That is a key. He's usually the general on the field. He's usually the one who is directing the second baseman, pitcher, first baseman, and third baseman. For instance, the shortstop should let the third baseman know with some verbal sign when the pitcher is throwing anything other than a fastball. It gives the third baseman an opportunity to take a step or two closer to the line if there is an off-speed pitch that a right-handed batter might be able to pull.

Another job of the shortstop is to let the pitcher know who will be covering second base if the ball is hit back to the pitcher with a runner on first. He also has to let the second baseman know who is going to cover second if the runner on first base attempts to steal. He needs to be able to read situations such as a possible hit-and-run—when, with a runner on base, the batter is trying to hit the ball and put it in play. When a runner might steal, the shortstop also should let the outfielders know that the pitcher is throwing something other than a fastball.

When I was making the call from second base—only because I was the more experienced middle infielder—I let the pitcher know who was covering second on the ball back to him, let the shortstop know who was covering second base if the runner stole, and I gave signs to the right fielder to let him know if the pitch was a breaking ball or a fastball. There's a lot that happens on the field that the average fan doesn't have a clue about. This game is so much fun for the guys who play it because they know the mental side of it and how much is involved in the strategy. That strategy is what makes the game a blast, because it's you trying to help outwit the other team, and when you win, you feel good about it.

Looking at the top shortstops in the league today such as Nomar Garciaparra, Omar Vizquel, Alex Rodriguez and Derek Jeter, they are quality guys and they know how to play the game. Each of those players has a strong arm, they all run well, and they are also very offensive-minded. But defense is what is going to set them apart from each other.

TAKING CHARGE OF THE GROUNDER

The shortstop is the player who can't wait for the groundball to come to him. Charging ground balls is often a do-or-die situation for a shortstop. Many shortstops like to come in as hard as they can, field the ball off their left foot and send the ball toward first base. If the ball is almost coming to a stop, the shortstop should try to field that ball with his bare hand and make a throw. If the ball has any bounce to it, he should use his glove and catch the ball before he throws it to first.

We often hear the phrase, "You have to charge the ball." I think that's an overused term, because there are certain grounders you can't charge. Good shortstops know when to charge and when not to. There are certain balls you just move in on. The high hop ball and the slow roller are the balls to charge. On those balls you should move in with your momentum going toward first base, catch the ball without your momentum stopping, and let your legs help you get the ball across the field to first.

MY TOUGHEST FUNDAMENTAL

"Learning how to go to the hole, backhand the ball, and throw to first base was the hardest fundamental for me."
—*Omar Vizquel, shortstop, Cleveland Indians*

On other grounders, keep your head up, watch the ball into your glove, fielding it with two hands (Figures 2-26, 2-26B and 2-26C). We hate to see a shortstop who catches the ball on the run all the time. He needs to be under control. Belanger once told me, "If you see a shortstop who can't set his feet after he fields a ground ball, I'll say that guy is not a good shortstop."

AP/WWP

Figure 2-26

Figure 2-26B

Figure 2-26C

PLAYING THE BUNT

If there's a runner on first base in a sacrifice bunt situation, the shortstop's responsibility is to cover second base. If there are runners on first and second, then his responsibility is going to depend on the play that the coaches call. On a special play he may be the guy who leaves early to cover third, with the third baseman charging toward home in hopes of fielding the bunt and throwing the ball to third base for the force out. Otherwise, on the routine bunts, the shortstop always goes to second base, while the second baseman covers first base.

PLAYING FOR TWO

As with second basemen, there are three types of groundballs shortstops must handle in a double-play situation—straight at you, to your left or to your right.

If the ball is hit directly at you, you want to be in a good, ready stance waiting to make a play. Keep your upper body aimed toward the incoming ball, slightly drop your left foot back to open your hips toward the second base bag, secure the ball in your glove, and make a chest-high throw to the second baseman. With your hips open, there is no wasted motion during the play, giving you a better chance to make a clean double play.

The player watches the ball into the glove and uses two hands to make the play.

You want to make sure you open your hips slightly and then make a good throw to the second baseman.

If the grounder is hit a few feet to your right, you should take shuffle steps to get in front of the ball, and then use the same approach as when the ball is directly at you.

If the ball is hit farther to your right, you want to make a cross-over step, get to the ball, backhand it off your right foot, keeping your weight on that right foot, then transfer your weight to come back over the top with a good throw to second.

If the grounder is hit toward the second base bag, you need to decide whether you're going to make a shuffle toss to the second baseman or if you're going to make the play yourself. Whenever you make an underhanded shuffle pass, be sure to keep the ball in plain view for the second baseman, and make a chest-high toss. You want to avoid bringing your arm all the way back to make the toss. When you take the play yourself, remember to yell, "I got it!" to let the second baseman know to clear out.

Be sure to watch the ball into your glove as you backhand it.

Keep the ball visible to the second baseman, even when you're making an underhand toss.

WHITE'S WORDS OF WISDOM

- Always use your glove when a groundball is bouncing.
- Use two hands when possible. We often see a shortstop come in and try to field the ball with one hand when he should come in, sit down and field through the ball with two hands.
- Slow rollers can be charged with one hand and thrown on the run.
- Always try to set your feet before you throw.

Third base

The third baseman is a player who really doesn't have to be fast but he has to be quick, and have a good first step. Brooks Robinson, who I thought was the greatest third baseman I ever saw play, wasn't a fast runner, but he had a good first step. He had soft hands and he had a "soft" body that he used to knock down balls. The third baseman is almost like a hockey goalie, because his main job oftentimes is not to catch the ball but to knock it down and give himself an opportunity to make a play.

He's got to be a guy who is daring. Sometimes you don't know if a hitter is going to bunt

George Brett

or swing away, so the third baseman has to be a guy with no fear of being in close and having the ball lined hard in his direction. A third baseman uses, in most cases, one of the larger gloves because he wants to knock the ball down.

A good third baseman should have some range and possess as strong an arm as the shortstop. It is often said that the shortstop's throw from the hole is one of the toughest plays to make in baseball. But if you take a third baseman

Bettmann/CORBIS

Brooks Robinson

who backhands the ball toward the line, his throw to first is going to be just as long as the throw from the shortstop in the hole. George Brett had a great arm at third, as did Mike Schmidt. Graig Nettles of the Yankees was another fine third baseman, as was Aurilio Rodriguez for Detroit.

Scott Brosius of the Yankees was extremely solid, as was Travis Fryman for the Cleveland Indians.

The better third basemen that I've seen have all had great arms to get the ball across the field. When hitters drag bunt down the line, you have to have a strong enough arm to come in and get the ball to first base, usually on the run.

Among today's third basemen, Joe Randa for the Royals has become a very good defensive player. When he first came to the major leagues in 1995, he nearly lobbed the ball over to first base, but he still got the runner out every time. Since then, his arm has actually gotten stronger and he throws the ball on the line. That's quite an improvement!

One of the up-and-coming stars at third is Troy Glaus for the Anaheim Angels. I think he's got all the tools to be a very good third baseman. Also, Scott Roland with St. Louis is one of the better young ones.

READY... SET...

The third baseman has to be ready for many possible plays. First, he has to know the hitter. He needs to know the angles. (That's where his quickness comes into play, because he doesn't really see what the shortstop and the second baseman see in terms of where the ball is.) The ball he gets is usually hooking because the hitter is pulling it either down the line or into the hole.

When the pitcher is winding up, the third baseman has to be in his pre-pitch stance, his ready stance, which is sort of like a tennis player waiting for a serve. He has to be on his toes, ready to move left or right, and be ready to see the ball in the hitting area out in front of the plate.

COVERING BUNTS FROM THE HOT CORNER

The first thing for a third baseman to remember on covering a bunt is that he has to make an accurate throw to first base. If the hitter is one who may drag bunt, the third baseman should get close to the line and angle himself so that he can make a throw to first. If he's not at an angle, he has to throw across his body so the ball won't sink back toward the runner. After you make the throw to first, you don't want to let your body fall off to the outside part of the field. A lot of times you'll see a third baseman come in, field the bunt with his bare hand, fire the ball to first and then fall flat out on his stomach. That's what you like to see because when that happens, the ball will go straight to first base. However, if you peel off as you are throwing, then that ball is going to run back into the runner, which could cause some problems for you and the first baseman.

There are certain keys that you look for to tell if the batter has bunting on his mind, even with no one on base. The third baseman should watch the head of the bat. If the head of the bat comes forward, then he should break toward the plate because the batter is either going to fake a bunt or he's going to bunt. If there is a runner on third base and you smell a squeeze play, watch the head of the bat along with the runner. If the runner breaks—which he has to do before the pitcher releases the ball in order for the squeeze to be successful—you break with him, and hopefully the batter will pop the ball up or miss it altogether.

When the runner is stealing third, straddle the bag, let the ball travel to the center of your body and then tag straight down.

CUT!

On a ball to the outfield, the third baseman's responsibility as a cut-off man is the same as the first baseman's. The first baseman and the third baseman also have to be able to read the situation. If, for instance, they feel that they have no chance to get the runner going to the plate, but feel they can get the batter-runner at second base, the corner guys have to be able to read that play, cut the ball off and make the play at second base.

PRIORITIES IN THE AIR

On pop ups the third baseman has priority over the catcher, the pitcher and anything in foul territory down the line, unless the shortstop calls him off. I like to see a third baseman catch balls that go over

The first and third basemen should give the outfielder a good target when lining up for the cutoff throw.

toward the stands, down the line a little bit, and by the dugout. At third base, you want to catch everything you can catch and make things as easy as possible for the pitcher and catcher.

COMMON MISTAKES

One of the most common mistakes that third basemen make is not knowing when to play in and when to play back. Also, they commonly have trouble recognizing a bunting situation versus a hitting situation. A big problem they have is not knowing how far to go to their left on ground balls, and they end up getting in the way of the shortstop. I think many third basemen have the same problem as first basemen on pop ups in foul territory, and not knowing how to position themselves for the ball.

WHITE'S WORDS OF WISDOM

- Obviously you want to catch every ball that you can catch, but on the balls that are hit directly at you, use your chest to keep the ball in front of you.
- Don't get on the side of a grounder and try to "Olé" the ball like a bull-fighter, which allows it to get by you. Usually when a ball is hit to an infielder and he gets on the side of it and just tries to wave his arm, it tells you that he didn't really have his heart in that particular play.
- You should field bunts that are rolling slowly with your bare hand. Balls that are bouncing should be fielded with the glove.
- Always be aggressive.

Outfield

The overall quality of an outfielder is first to have the athletic ability to be a good outfielder. But to me, the best quality of an outfielder is the ability to manage the game—knowing how to charge the ball with a good approach, being able to release the ball with accuracy and quickness, and not relying on total arm strength. Most third base coaches stop runners based on how the outfielder approaches the ball, how long it took him to get rid of the ball, and his accuracy in throwing it. You can have a cannon, but if the third base coach knows that you are not accurate with that strong arm, he is still going to challenge you with his runner.

Outfielders have to know the situation, when to try to throw runners out, and when not to try to throw them out. Regardless, always plan to hit the cut-off man. Always keep the double play in order when you don't have a chance to throw a guy out at the plate. Those are some things that a coach likes to see in an outfielder.

Each outfield position has specific characteristics, especially as a player advances from little league, but there are certain qualities that a coach likes to see in every outfielder. The most ideal is arm strength. All good outfielders should have strong arms. The ability to read hitters and position themselves accordingly is also important.

Obviously, we would like for all of our outfielders to have good speed, strong arms and be able to do all the smart things like positioning for hitters, hitting the cut-off man, and things like that, but it doesn't always happen that way. On many teams, the weakest arm is in left field because it's closer to home plate. It is nice if the center fielder has a strong arm, but he is mainly there for his all-around defense. Usually the center fielder is the best athlete, because of his speed, agility and ability to cover the most ground in the outfield. Most center fielders don't throw out many runners. Usually the strongest arm is in right field.

Most times, the slowest player is in left field. Again, that's predicated on arm strength. You can have your slowest player in right field if he has the stronger arm. Left field is usually reserved for the player who is not the best athlete and doesn't have the strongest arm.

The center fielder is usually the leader of the outfield because of priorities. He's the one who has priority over everyone in the outfield on fly balls. But he also has to realize his territory. You can only go so far before you infringe on your teammate's area, so the center fielder has to be aware of where he is positioned. He is the player who must remember how to play hitters and help position the other outfielders. Kirby Puckett with Minnesota was a good leader in center field. He was pretty animated in the outfield, but you could see him helping guys move around.

Throughout the 1970s and 1980s, we had quite a few good outfielders in Kansas City. The key thing I would note that made them all successful is not that they all had strong arms, but they were accurate. Fundamentally, they were hitting cut-off men and doing the things they were supposed to do. They also paid a lot of attention to positioning and being able to read the situation to see what the hitter was trying to do. We had Willie Wilson, who had a lot of speed but didn't have a strong arm, in left field as a Gold Glove Award winner. Because he charged the ball so well, he was right behind the shortstop when he threw the ball. He later moved to center field. Even though Willie didn't win any Gold Gloves there, he played as good a center field as I've ever seen. Unfortunately, he didn't have the strength in his arm to throw runners out going from first to third, or scoring from second on a base hit.

Willie Wilson

Willie's predecessor in center field was Amos Otis, who had a strong arm but didn't quite have the speed of Willie. But Amos could play and position himself with the best of them. Amos was the most fundamental outfielder I've played with. He won three Gold Glove Awards. Al Cowens, on the other hand, had good speed in right field and had the strongest arm of them all. He also won a Gold Glove Award.

The thing about all those guys was that they were accurate with their throws. I think that's what made them the great players that they were.

Today's game at the major-league level has several fundamentally sound outfielders. One of the best is Jermaine Dye, with whom I worked in Kansas City. Bernie Williams, Ken Griffey Jr., Kenny Lofton and Andruw Jones are all very good fundamental outfielders. There are a lot of guys out there who bring everything to the table in the outfield.

MY TOUGHEST FUNDAMENTAL

"I didn't play the outfield until 1989, when I was in Double-A. My whole life I had been an infielder, mainly second base and shortstop. So, when I moved to the outfield, I didn't know how to play the position. Everything was tough for me to learn out there. I think I was able to adapt to it because I had been an infielder, and there are a lot of similarities if you have the fundamentals."
—*Brian McRae, who played 10 major-league seasons with Kansas City, the Chicago Cubs, the New York Mets, Colorado and Toronto*

GETTING READY

The pre-pitch and ready stance for an outfielder is going to depend on the player. Each player should be treated as an individual because some players can have their hands on their knees but they aren't really resting on their knees. They can be in that position with the weight on the balls of their feet, able to anticipate what the hitter is trying to do, and be ready to get a good jump.

**A good ready stance
for an outfielder.**

Some outfielders like to start from a dead stop, while others like to creep forward a little bit to get some momentum, and then react to the ball.

Regardless, the player should have his weight on the balls of his feet with some movement in his body, whether he's walking in place with little tiny steps or using a little swing in his hips. It is better to have some movement on the pitch rather than starting dead still. The longer you're still, the tighter you're going to get and you won't react the way you should.

Once a pitcher starts his motion, everyone on the field should do something to get ready for the ball being hit, whether it is to creep in a few steps and get set, or to drop down a little bit in your knees to get set. As you watch a major league game, on each pitch you'll see one guy break one way and one guy break another way. That's part of their anticipation of what's going to happen when the hitter swings the bat.

As far as an outfielder's placement, coaches are responsible for positioning the outfielders on certain hitters. That was one of my duties as the outfielders' coach. I took the players through the lineup once, and then they usually made their own adjustments after that. Sometimes I'd remind them late in the game when to throw the ball to second base to keep the double play in order. We tried to warn them late in the game when to play deeper if we had the lead to make sure that if anything went over their head that it was either going to hit the wall or go out of the ballpark. We tried not to give up the double and instead tried to force three singles for every run our opponents got.

MY BEST ADVICE

"Don't get bored in the outfield. Play it like an infielder—be prepared on every pitch. Expect the ball to be hit to you. And don't think that you're in the outfield because you're a bad player. That's not necessarily the case."
—*Brian McRae, who mainly played center field in the major leagues for 10 seasons with five teams*

JUMP ON IT!

It is crucial to get good jumps in the outfield because if you don't, it could mean a single becomes a double, or a double becomes a triple. Your first three steps are the most important steps you're going to take when going for a ball. You have to be on the balls of your feet and you have to be able to react at the moment the ball is struck. If your first three steps are legitimate hard steps, then chances are you're going to cover a lot of ground and have an opportunity to make a tough catch. If your first three steps are lazy and slow, then chances are good that you are not going to make the tough play.

TAKING CHARGE OF THE GROUNDER

When a ball is on the ground in the outfield, you should avoid getting down on one knee to field it. If there is no one on base, try to come in and react to the ball like an infielder. Get in front of the ball, bend your knees, watch the ball, field through it with your left foot for right-handed throwers (or right foot for left-handed throwers) and then throw it in to second base.

If there is a runner on first base who probably won't try to go to third on a ground ball to the outfield, come in and also field that ball like an infielder, then get it to the cut-off man. If the runner

Fielding a grounder with a runner on first who probably won't try to advance to third.

may try to advance from first to third, make a hard charge on the ball, then field it—if you're a right-handed thrower try to field the ball just inside your left foot, and if you're a left hander, field it just inside your right foot—by going through the ball and into your crow hop.

You want to try to limit your fielding to three steps. You catch the ball on one step, crow hop on step two, then throw the ball on your third step. If you're a left hander, the steps would be right, left, right. If you're right

Fielding a grounder with no runners on base.

handed, the steps would be left, right, left. Try to cut everything down to three steps rather than four or five steps.

CAMPING UNDER THE FLY

Once a fly ball goes up, the proper thing for an outfielder to do is get behind the ball, and as it is coming down, anticipate where you need to be, and try to catch it with two hands, preferably over your throwing shoulder. If you have a tag-up situation, get behind the ball and take little choppy steps to help get your momentum ready for a throw to your cut-off man. Once the ball gets to your glove, you want to be able to move through that ball into your crow hop and have the throw on the way to the base ahead of where the runner is tagging.

At an early age especially, you should try to teach kids to catch everything with two hands, knowing that the more confident the player gets in his abilities, the more he is going to develop his own style. For major-league players catching with one hand, as long as they're not dropping balls and as long as they're in the proper fielding position, we're not going to say anything. When you field with two hands, remember that you can't shield your eyes with the glove. As I mentioned earlier in the chapter, you always need to keep your glove just off to the side of your head, so you can actually get a clear vision of the ball with your eyes.

HITTING THE CUT-OFF MAN

There are several important reasons you hit the cut-off man on throws back to the infield. If you hit the first cut-off man, your defense has a chance to throw the runner out trying to score or reach the next base. If you miss the cut-off man, your chances of having a play on the runner are pretty slim.

Hitting the cut-off man also stops base runners. If the batter gets a base hit and runs hard around first with the idea of possibly going to second, and that throw from the cut-off man is down about head high, then the coach is going to tell the batter-runner to stay at first base. If that incoming throw is high over the cut-off man's head, then the third-base coach is going to let that runner go. Those are very important reasons why you always need to hit the cut-off man.

Ideally, you want to throw the ball through the cut-off man—instead of to him—about head high. If you want to make it even easier on him, try to place the throw on the glove side of his head. A nearly perfect throw such as that will eliminate time during the relay, and will give your team a better chance at getting the runner. If the throw is off the line, the cut-off man should move to the glove side to receive the throw.

THROWING FOR OUTFIELDERS

Even though throwing will be discussed more thoroughly in chapter 5, it is extremely important for an outfielder to always attempt to use the proper grip on the baseball. Ideally, you want to use four seams—meaning, when the ball is rotating after your throw, all four seams are spinning backwards.

A four-seam spin, when thrown overhand, helps ensure the ball will go as straight as possible instead of tailing away from the target. If you are having trouble gripping that way, while you're sitting on the bench toss a baseball up in the air and get used to just catching it, rotating it to the four-seam grip and get a feel for it that way. Players can also do that drill at home while studying or just sitting around. Practicing the grip is a good way to know that if you come up with a ball in the middle of your crow hop, you can always maneuver to that four-seam grip.

Then on your throw you want to come over the top and finish with a good follow through.

An outfielder should make an overhand throw and finish with a good follow through.

COVER YOUR TEAMMATES

A theme of this chapter is the importance of different defensive positions backing up each other. The outfield is no exception. In fact, the outfielders have many responsibilities when it comes to backing up plays. When outfielders consider plays they need to back up, their first responsibility is to back each other up. Balls hit in right center field or left center field are especially concerning. We hate to see an outfielder dive for a ball toward the center of the field, miss it, and then have to get up and chase his own ball. The outfielder not going for the dive should be ready in case the ball goes by. That also holds true if there is a ball that is hit toward the wall, and the outfielder might try to jump for it. The other closest outfielder should be in position to take the ball off the wall if the player who's trying to make the catch does not catch it (Figure 2-37).

Figure 2-37

A base hit to left field is automatically a potential double, so the right fielder has to position himself for a throw from the left fielder to second base. Many times that throw is over the head of the second baseman, so the right fielder has the responsibility to back up that play. The right fielder has to anticipate if his team has a catcher who likes to throw behind a runner at first base; he always has to be ready to back up that play. He needs to be in position for an overthrow at first base on an infield play. The right fielder also has to be ready if there is a potential double play where the third baseman or the short-stop throws the ball to the second baseman. He has to be coming hard to back that play up in case there is an overthrow at the bag.

The center fielder has to be ready for overthrows from the catcher on steal attempts, and on errant throws by the pitcher on pick-off plays at second. If there is a runner on first and there is a ground ball to the first baseman or the second baseman, the left fielder is responsible for backing that play up at second base. If there's a first-and-third situation where the right fielder is making a throw to third base, then the left fielder comes up the line in that direction in case there is an overthrow and the ball gets down the left field line. He needs to anticipate a pick-off play at third base and also a possible over-throw from the catcher on a steal attempt at third.

Outfielders have many responsibilities. Backing up plays is definitely an overlooked responsibility. If you hustle, even when the ball is not hit to you, you could help save your team a run.

MY TOUGHEST FUNDAMENTAL

"Coming in on the ball with an infielder coming back was most difficult for me. As an outfielder, you have to make that judgment call sooner than you think. Especially when you have speedy infielders like Frank coming back, you have to know if you're going to call them off or let them take it."
—*Amos Otis, outfielder, and my teammate during 1973-83*

PLAYING THE FENCE

In order to play the fence effectively, you first have to be an outfielder who is not afraid to run into the wall. One of the keys to playing the fence is the warning track. Knowing when you're leaving grass and going on to the track and how many steps you have on the track before you hit the wall is vital. If you're not familiar with a particular field's warning track size, go out there before a game and step it off. Count the number of steps you have on the track before hitting the wall, then put that number in the back of your mind until

Figure 2-38

you need it. You'll find that with the padded walls today, outfielders are a little more aggressive on the fences. A lot of them will hit the wall, or climb up and try to hold the top part of the fence to try to make that great catch.

The key to playing the wall is that when you get back there, feel for the wall with your bare hand, as you continue to concentrate on the ball. Then, when you jump, make sure you jump straight up and not into the wall. You'll see a lot of guys who will get up against the wall and when they go to make their jump for the ball, they'll jump backwards into the wall versus jumping straight up. When you don't go straight up, you hurt the height of your jump, and decrease your chances of catching the ball. The key is to have that bare hand out there so you can know just where you are on the wall and then you can time your jump from there (Figure 2-38).

MY BEST ADVICE

"To be a good outfielder, you have to have a determination and will power to be the best. Things will come easier that way. You have to work at it. You can't go out and take a few fly balls, and think you're finished. You have to see a lot of fly balls, line drives hit right at you, balls hit off the wall, and so on. If you have the dedication, the game will be simpler for you."
—*Amos Otis, five-time All-Star outfielder*

WHITE'S WORDS OF WISDOM

- Never miss the cut-off man.
- Never try to throw a runner out that you can't throw out.
- Always assume that a runner's going to challenge you for the next base. He's looking at your body language and the type of ball that's hit.
- Always have good intent to come in, get the ball, and then get rid of it quickly.
- Never lob the ball back to the cut-off man because there are some aggressive base runners who will take advantage of that.
- Always communicate with the other outfielders.
- Always communicate with the infielders.
- Always call for the ball loudly, yelling, "I got it! I got it! I got it!"
- Always calculate the next situation in your mind before it happens so when the ball is hit, you are able to react without thinking about it.
- Always remember your back-up responsibilities.

The battery

The most specialized area on the field, which has a completely different set of rules, is the battery—the pitcher and catcher. Obviously, this is the area that controls the flow of the game, and usually the outcome. Even though the strategies, rules and intricacies of the pitcher and catcher could fill an entire book, the following basic fundamental rules still apply.

Catcher

The catcher can do a lot of things to control the flow of the game. He is responsible for helping the pitcher through the tough times (and tough batters) in an inning. The catcher is there to remind the pitcher how he is supposed to work each hitter. He calls the pitches and pitch locations.

An ideal catcher has a strong, accurate throwing arm, which helps defend against a stolen base. We like to see a catcher who is tough physically and tough mentally—one who can remember hitter by hitter, and at the same time not be afraid to block home plate when he's trying to tag out charging runners. A good catcher is going to help you win. He's usually quick with his feet, like Ivan Rodriguez.

Rodriguez has a strong throwing arm and is very quick with the ball. He would be the ideal example of what you'd like to see in a catcher—a guy who can hit, throw, and play defense with the ability to come out on bunt plays, field the ball and throw to first base.   Even though the ideal catcher has a strong arm, it's not absolutely necessary.

AP/WWP

Ivan Rodriguez

During the 1970s, Thurman Munson for the Yankees didn't have a very strong arm, but he was such a good athlete that he was extremely quick at getting rid of the ball. Many times the runners would be tagged out two or three feet down the line toward first base because the ball got there so fast. He was very quick with his hands and his feet. To consistently throw runners out at second, catchers need soft hands to be able to make the transfer and then have quick feet to make the throw.

Most people would tell you that when base runners run, they don't steal on the catcher, they steal on the pitcher. It's nice to have a strong arm, but if the pitcher is not going to give the catcher an opportunity to throw the runner out, it really doesn't help. So you'll see a lot of managers who opt to go with the catcher with the average arm, but who can call the game. Good game calling is very important to most managers and pitchers. There are many catchers who have strong arms but they don't call good games.

The catcher, in general, is the player who gets the pitchers through tough times and remembers what pitches are working and which ones are not work-ing. He will periodically come to the pitch that's not working to see if the pitcher has picked it up yet.

He's got to do a little bit of everything—he runs the game, he reminds everyone how many outs have been recorded in the inning, he looks at the defense and then he tries to pitch according to how the defense is playing.

MY TOUGHEST FUNDAMENTAL

"Catching is a very demanding position physically. I was a converted catcher, so I knew what I was getting into. All the fundamentals are difficult—the blocking, the throwing, the footwork that goes into the various drills. But, for me, the most difficult thing about catching was the mental part—knowing my pitchers and the opposing hitters. This to me is the last skill that the catcher masters. The physical fundamentals come quicker than the mental side."

—*Jamie Quirk, who played 18 seasons in the major leagues, mostly at catcher*

BLOCKING THE PLATE

One of the key things that a catcher must do is be adept at blocking errant pitches. The catcher turns those into saves.

Pitchers appreciate a catcher who can take care of home plate. They like knowing that they can throw the ball in the dirt and it is going to be blocked and not be scored as a wild pitch. They need that confidence in their catcher that they don't have to throw a perfect strike every time.

SERVING AS A BACKSTOP...IN OTHER WAYS

On a ground ball to the infield with nobody on base, the catcher should hustle down from home plate to back up the first baseman. Catchers basically are behind-the-plate people, but they do have some responsibilities in backing up.

MY BEST ADVICE

"I think the best advice is to want to catch, because catching is hard to find. If you really like baseball and want to pursue it at a higher level, catching is the way to go. There is a shortage of catching, so get out there and catch."

—*Jamie Quirk, who has been a major league coach for Kansas City, Texas and Colorado*

WHITE'S WORDS OF WISDOM

- A catcher absolutely has to be a player who blocks balls in the dirt.
- A catcher should be able to field his position well on pop ups around the plate and on bunts out in front of the plate.
- A catcher can never be afraid. He needs to be able to block the runner off the plate when the runner is trying to score.
- A catcher should never let a ball get by him with runners on base.
- A catcher should always be in a position where he can move side to side or drop straight down on blocked balls. Sometimes catchers let their rear ends get too low below their knees and then if the ball is off to their right or left they don't shift well, and those balls tend to get by.
- Always know your range. Don't go too far down the first and third base lines on pop ups. Know how far you can go.
- Never try to throw a runner out when you know you really don't have a chance to get him. It only leads to a bad throw and usually the runner advances one more base.

Pitcher

Defensively, pitchers are commonly known as people you try to keep away from every play you can keep them from, especially pop ups. However, there are certain balls that are hit right over the mound that the corner guys can't get to that the pitcher can catch. We encourage the pitcher to catch those balls, but he has to make sure that he yells loudly enough that the other infielders hear him call for the ball.

I don't think many pitchers are given credit for being good athletes. There must have been some bad fielding pitchers in the past somewhere, because everyone tries to keep them out of plays. Coaches try to keep pitchers out of run-down plays and away from catching pop ups. Defensively, pitchers are known as helpers more than anything else.

One of the plays that pitchers are taught most often is covering first base on a grounder to the right side of the infield. Sometimes they are so engrossed in pitching that if there is a ground ball to first, they don't get off the mound fast enough to cover, and the runner is safe at first base. The pitcher has to be conscious that a ball could be hit back to the mound, so once he releases the pitch, he should be in a good fielding position. Because of the way some pitchers throw, they don't actually get back into a good fielding position. If a pitcher ends up in a fielding position after releasing the pitch, that definitely helps the cause.

After the pitch is delivered to home plate, the follow-through should put the pitcher in a fielding position similar to all the infielders. He should end up square to home plate, knees slightly bent, ready to react to the ball hit back to the middle, whether it be a line drive or a hard ground ball left or right.

MY TOUGHEST FUNDAMENTAL

"As a younger player, it was difficult for me to learn my responsibilities as a pitcher after the ball left my hand, especially covering first base on a ball hit to my left side [the first-base side]. That's the most difficult thing to do con-sistently as a young pitcher be-cause your thoughts are so in-grained on making the pitch and getting hitters out that, at times, you tend to be a spectator. After taking a great deal of pitcher's fielding practice, I was able to get over that hump. I came up in an organization—the Chi-cago Cubs—that drilled all of the defensive fundamentals for pitchers. Now when a ball is hit to my left, I instinctively run to first base."

—*Jamie Moyer, pitcher, who from 1996-2000 had the major league's third-highest winning percentage (.673)*

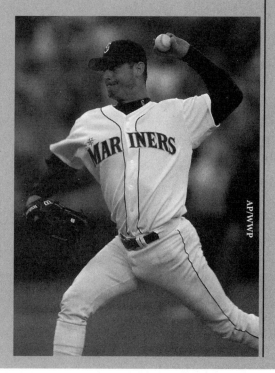

AP/WWP

MY TOUGHEST FUNDAMENTAL

"The toughest fundamental for me was keeping my rhythm during a game."
—*Gaylord Perry, Hall of Fame pitcher, who retired with more than 300 wins and 3,500 strikeouts*

AP/WWP

With a man on first base, always check with the shortstop and the second baseman to see who's covering the base if the ball is hit back to the mound. If there is no one on base, then the first baseman communicates with the pitcher before every hitter to know that he's covering first on a grounder to that side of the infield. Pitchers also have to be able to field bunts down the first and third base lines, and in front of the mound. You have to know who the fielders are on bunt plays and pick-off attempts. You also need to know all of the different pick-off plays at each of the bases. You need to anticipate a possible squeeze play so you can try to field that bunt.

PITCHERS ON POP-UPS

Whether pitchers should try to catch a pop up depends on how high the ball is going. If it's not very high, then we encourage the pitchers to catch the ball. Like other fielders, they must call the ball and catch it. If the ball is really high, then it depends on whether it's to the left side or right side of the mound. If the ball is high and to the left or right, then one of the infielders should go for it.

When a pop up is down the first or third base line, or somewhere around the mound, the pitcher's job is to act as the general to decide whose name he is going to call out. Once he hears a player call for the ball, then his job is to keep repeating that player's name while trying to keep another infielder from getting involved.

BACK UP YOUR INFIELDERS

One big responsibility for a pitcher is to back up certain infielders on various plays. Pitchers need to back up home plate on a base hit when runners are on base. They need to get deep behind home plate so they can adjust to the throw and keep the ball from rattling around back there and allowing the hitter to take an extra base. Pitchers also need to back up third base. Again, they should get deep enough that if the ball gets by the third baseman, they have a chance to adjust and go left or right to try to cut the ball off.

In a situation where a pop up goes into short center field, and both the second baseman and the shortstop go for it, then a lot of teams will have their pitcher cover second base. Or if there is a base hit to left field, where the shortstop goes out and the second baseman is at the bag, some pitchers will back up the second baseman. That all depends on the pitcher, how athletic he is and how well he remembers where he needs to go.

MY BEST ADVICE

"As a pitcher, be able to throw strikes. The best pitch in baseball is a strike; I don't care what type of pitch it is. You need to keep the flow of the game moving, and you need to keep your defense in the game. The way to do that is to throw strikes. If you can throw your fastball for a strike, there's no reason to learn any other pitch. Growing up, I had a lot of success as a pitcher but if I knew then what I know now, I would've thrown a lot more fastballs and tried to utilize my fastball more."

— *Jamie Moyer, pitcher, who finished the 2001 campaign with a record of 20-6; he became the oldest pitcher—38 at the time—in history to win 20 games for the first time*

WHITE'S WORDS OF WISDOM

- As a pitcher, don't assume that you're a bad fielder. Don't assume that you're never going to catch any type of pop up and don't give in to the thinking that pitchers aren't good athletes.
- Always hustle off the mound and be at first base for the throw from the first baseman on a grounder to that side of the infield.
- Always know who is going to be covering the bag at second base when there's a runner on first.
- Don't assume on a pop up that one infielder hears you over someone else's yelling. You've got to get off the mound, get close to the play and make sure that all the infielders involved can hear you.
- Always remember to back up a play. A lot of times pitchers get so frustrated that they make a late reaction to the play and forget to back up.

Summing up defense

Regardless of your position on the field, you really have to take pride in your defense. Defense wins ballgames. Defense makes good pitching. Pitchers appreciate good defense. They feel much more confident pitching knowing that players are out there who have confidence in their defense, take pride in it and work at it. If you have consistent defense, day in and day out, your team will win many games. It goes back to your work ethic, your work habits and knowing what everybody does on every play.

You should always want the ball to be hit to you all the time. Once the ball is hit to you, you have to know what you are going to do with it. Finally, you need the will to be better. Dedicate yourself to improving your defense and being the best defensive player possible.

Chapter 3

Fundamental Hitting

Hitting a baseball is probably the single most difficult thing to do in sports—in any sport. (That's encouraging, isn't it?) I think that when most fans come to the game, they like to see as much offense as possible. Offense is not only exciting to watch, but it is what keeps players on the team. You can only carry so many defensive players; someone has to drive in runs. The old adage sometimes seems true—you can shake a glove out of a tree any time, but good hitters are hard to find.

Hitting starts with good hand-eye coordination, along with good balance and being able to see the ball out of a pitcher's hand, reading the pitches and using the whole field to hit. I have not extensively studied science, but think for a minute about the physics of hitting a baseball. You're taking a long, skinny, round object (the bat) and trying to make solid contact with another small, round object (the ball). To further complicate matters, the two objects are traveling in opposite directions! On top of that, not all balls are coming in straight—there are those curve balls, sliders, knuckleballs, etc. Baseball people sometimes wish that fans understood just how difficult it is to hit a baseball. For a pitcher it is all about breaking the timing of the hitter. You have a pitcher who throws 90 miles an hour, but he also throws a change up that's 80 mph and a curve ball that's 75 mph. Hitting involves a series of constant adjustments that you have to make with your brain, your hands, your eyes, and so forth.

As a player, I worked as hard as I could on my hitting skills. Early in my career, I bunted a lot and I hit and ran a lot. (When you hit and run, the base runner at first steals and you try to hit the ball hard on the ground and hope that the second baseman or shortstop is covering the bag.) I had good bat control and I moved the ball around very well. It wasn't until 1983 when I moved to the middle of the order that I got some protection from the No. 4 hitter. Then, whenever I had a count of 3-1 or 3-2, I got a fastball and I was able to hit more for power.

Early in my major-league career, my time at the plate was spent trying to get used to the pitchers in the league. That wasn't easy at all. I really had to work at it through constant practice. Being a right-handed hitter, I tried to hit everything to right field, trying to make sure I saw the ball. Then as I matured a little bit and started learning the pitchers in the league and listening to my coaches and some of my teammates—being surrounded by so many good hitters—I started to get better.

Over the course of time, I reached a comfort level. That's the way it is for most players. I think you reach a point where you feel like you can adjust to nearly anything that the pitcher is trying to do to you. That comes through trial and error, and through success and confidence. Once you set that consistent performance as a hitter year to year, your confidence builds.

One of the toughest pitchers for me to hit was Nolan Ryan, not just because of how hard he threw the ball—he threw it anywhere from 97 to 100 miles an hour—but because it was hard to distinguish his breaking ball from his fastball. Then there were pitchers such as Larry Gura and Jamie Moyer, who didn't necessarily throw hard but they changed speeds very well and kept me off balance. Most hitters want to face the guy who just brings straight heat because they don't have to change anything in their swing; they just have to make sure the pitch is a strike. The pitchers who can change speeds and throw the ball on both sides of the plate are tough because they can break your timing. You don't stay in a strong hitting position very long against those pitchers.

Most hitters today concentrate more on their offense than their defense. That isn't a fault of the players but rather the way the mentality of the game has changed. In the past, guys such as Hank Aaron, Mickey Mantle and Willie Mays were complete, all-around players. Today if you can hit, teams will try to find a place to put you.

EVERY PLACE IS IMPORTANT

The general feeling with managers and coaches, especially in little league, is that the best hitters are at the top of a line-up, and everybody else falls in behind. As someone who has hit at nearly every spot in a line-up, I can say that isn't altogether true. Here is my breakdown of batters' responsibilities in the lineup:

1. The lead-off hitter is a player that you would prefer to have speed. He doesn't necessarily have to be a power player, but definitely a player who can hit singles and doubles. He needs to have a lot of patience at the plate, and also be able to steal bases for you.

2. This is a guy who can have power, can hit doubles. He needs to be patient, because if he has a base stealer on the base in front of him, he has wait to let the player steal second so he can hit behind the runner and move him over to third base. The No. 2 hitter also is a player with good bat control, and preferably he can bunt.

3. The No. 3 hitter, some people feel, should be the best hitter on your ball club. I don't necessarily agree that he has to be the best hitter on the ball club, but he does have to be a player who can put the ball in play and doesn't strike out much. He basically needs to be able to drive in runs.

4. This is typically a power hitter, a player who can drive in the first three hitters.

5. The No. 5 player fits the same profile as the No. 4 hitter.

6. The No. 6 hitter can also fall in that category.

7. This batter typically is a player who might be a high strike-out player. In the seven spot, you don't worry about him, you just let him do what he does best and hopefully he drives in some runs for you.

8. Typically your Nos. 8 and 9 hitters are the players who have pretty good bat control. They lack a lot of power, but they can bunt and run. In the National League, the No. 8 hitter would be ahead of the pitcher, so his job is to try to get on base and not let the pitcher have to lead off an inning. He, by far, is pitched to tougher in the National League than in the American League. In the American League's designated hitter system, the No. 8 hitter can be a good hitter and a productive hitter.

9. The No. 9 hitter is basically the same as the No. 8 hitter. In the National League, this is usually where the pitcher hits. I felt most comfortable in the third, fourth, fifth and sixth spots because I was getting some protection there. In 1985, for instance, around me were George Brett and Hal McRae, then we had Steve Balboni in the seventh spot with 36 home runs. With McRae behind me, it made a big difference how teams pitched to me. They would rather let me beat them than let Hal beat them. I enjoyed it when I went down to the middle of the order, because that's when my power numbers started to go up.

TEXTBOOK BASEBALL

I'm a fan of what is considered "textbook baseball." For instance, when you get a runner on first with nobody out, you try to move him to scoring position, through a sacrifice or hit and run. Accomplishing that is the fundamental responsibility of the hitter at the plate at that time. In another example, if there is a runner on first and he's being held on, there is going to be a big hole between first and second. If the hitter is not a big power hitter, then I encourage him to hit the ball in that big hole to try to create a first-and-third situation.

Hitters need to learn how to be selective when there is a man on third and and an opportunity for a sacrifice fly. The batter's responsibility is to try to get a pitch that is sort of up in the zone so that he can hit a fly ball and try to get that run in. If there's a man on second, then the responsibility of the hitter is to try to get the runner to third by either bunting the ball to third or first; hitting a ground ball to first or second; or driving a ball deep enough into right field or center field so that the runner might score. There are fundamental responsibilities of the hitter that need to be taught, have to be stressed, and should be followed up on all the time.

MY BEST ADVICE

"In terms of baseball, learning fundamentals is the most important thing in the world for young players. They even have to understand what a baseball does in flight. They have to understand the baseball bat—what it can do, how to hit with two strikes, and so on. They need to learn the whys and hows. Once you have the ability to execute, you can play anywhere. But when the manager gives you the bunt sign, you have to execute. Look at it this way: if you have a tough subject in school, and you've really prepared well for the final exam, you've drilled yourself over and over, you have no fear. But if you've been slacking off, you're going to have a problem. There's poor execution in the major leagues today because players haven't been drilled over and over in the fundamentals."

—*Syd Thrift, long-time major league scout and baseball executive, and the director of the defunct Royals Baseball Academy*

Mechanics

BAT SELECTION

The size of your bat can definitely help or hurt you as you develop your hitting techniques. Your hand size matters. What kind of feel do you want in your hands? Do you want the feel of a fat bat in your hands or do you want the feel of a skinny handle? You have to decide which you like best. Once you select a bat, then you have to look at the head of the bat and decide if you want a skinny head or a big head. Once you decide on your handle size and the head size, then it is just a matter of how strong you are and how many ounces you want the bat to weigh. The bat I used was a model P72, which was 35 inches long and weighed 32 ounces.

Younger players often feel that the bigger the bat, the more power it will generate. You have to understand that your power doesn't come from the weight of your bat, it comes from how much bat speed you can generate in the hitting zone. If you have a lighter bat that you can whip through the zone, then obviously with any kind of strength, you're going to hit the ball harder than you would if you have a heavier bat that slugs through the zone. It takes more to swing a heavier bat, so chances are that if your bat is too heavy, your shoulders are going to drop and you're going to swing up. Then you won't have what you most need—crucial bat speed.

GRIPPING THE BAT

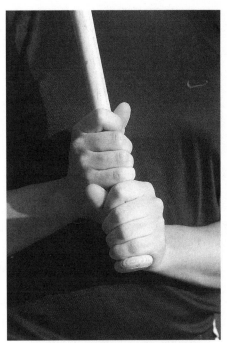

To grip the bat, you want to line up your knuckles. Doing that will give you more flexibility in your wrists and will enable your wrists to work as you "throw" the bat head toward the pitch. Having your knuckles lined up properly will help your shoulders remain level, and give you a good downward-to-level swing. If you choke the bat to where either your big knuckles are lined up or your big knuckles are lined with little knuckles, you create tension in your forearms, which forces you to drop your back shoulder and takes away your good downward-to-level swing.

When you grip a bat too tightly it increases tension. And when you create tension, you have absolutely no bat speed, the swing is not fluid, and therefore it's slow and it drags through the zone. A loose grip is fine, but at the point of contact with the ball, your grip should firm up.

Lining up your knuckles properly will give your wrists more flexibility in the swing.

Even though I gripped the bat on the knob throughout most of my career, I did choke up during my first year. Whether or not you choke up on the bat is up to you. The main reason you might want to choke up is for bat control. By choking up you're not trying to hit the ball out of the ballpark; you're trying to hit a line drive or ground ball. If you don't have a lot of strength and you hold the bat on the knob, it's more difficult to control the bat exactly the way you would like. So if you choke up, you have more control and you don't feel like you have to drop back your shoulder to generate bat speed.

THE STANCE

First and foremost when you step up to the plate, you need to know where to stand in the batter's box. Your feet have to be comfortable. You need to have good balance and rhythm. For most hitters, their feet are a little wider than shoulder-width apart and they have a little flexion in their knees, with their head turned toward the pitcher. You want to keep your shoulders square. You also want good plate coverage.

A good test to make sure you have complete plate coverage is to step in the box, extend your arms and lower the bat to where it's touching home plate.

A good, general ready stance.

If the far edge of home plate lands on the end of your bat, then you're a good distance from home plate. If the bat extends beyond the plate, then you need to step away until the end of the bat touches the far edge. If your bat doesn't reach the far side of the plate, then you need to step closer until the end of it does touch the far edge of home. Deciding how deep you want to be in the box, or how far up you want to be, is generally your personal preference. Stand in the batter's box wherever you feel most comfortable. Usually, I stood fairly deep in the box because I wanted to see the ball a little bit longer.

That was an especially helpful strategy against hard throwers like Nolan Ryan. However, when I faced a left-handed off-speed pitcher like Tommy John or a knuckle-baller like Charlie Hough, I moved up in the box. Then when I faced guys who threw a good slider, like Fergie Jenkins, I stood more even with the plate because I wanted to hit the pitch before it broke downward. With those "junk" pitchers, I used a two-strike approach. (That's the approach you use when there are two strikes and you spread out your stance and let the pitcher throw the ball, then you react to what the pitch is doing.)

At a young level, where pitchers are mainly throwing straight fastballs, you should stand toward the back of the box where you can see the ball longer. That will help improve your hand-eye coordination. Also, from the back of the box you shouldn't feel like you have to rush as much to hit the ball.

My stance changed considerably throughout my career. Actually, it changed a lot! When I played, my strength was on the inside pitch, so I usually stood right on the plate—very close to the plate—to help make sure I got an inside pitch. When pitchers started throwing me outside pitches, I would have to go with the pitch and hit it to right field in order to get the pitcher to come back inside.

Baseball is a game of constant adjustments, which includes knowing what the pitcher wants to throw you versus what you want him to throw. In order to get him to do what you want him to do, you have to hit his pitch a couple times to bring him back to your preference.

READY

Every hitter is going to have a different ready position. Basically, you have to start with a comfortable stance with both eyes on the pitcher. In a "conventional" stance, most hitters can't get their head turned enough to where both eyes are on the pitcher. Because of that, many hitters will open up their stance so that both eyes are on the pitcher.

When you're waiting on the pitcher to start his motion for the pitch, you want to be as relaxed as possible. The best way to make sure you're relaxed is not to stand like a statue in the box. If you're in your ready stance before the pitcher has even looked in to the catcher for the signals, you won't be relaxed. The longer that you're in your ready stance, the more tense you are going to be. That tension with no body movement will translate to a hurried body swing instead of a fluid hand-eye swing where you trust your hands to do the work for you. You want to stay relaxed and loose as long as you can, including your legs, arms and fingers. The point of contact in your swing is where everything in your body gets firm.

If you're in the ready position too long, and you feel your body get tight, the only way to relieve that is to either take a quick check swing or call time out and step out of the box for a few seconds. Then you're ready to go again. That same principle applies to fielding. If you're ready too soon, you usually shift your weight to your heels. In defense, as with hitting, you need to be in sync with the pitcher.

When you're waiting for the pitch, the way to keep yourself relaxed is to always have a little movement in your midsection. This back-and-forth movement is very slight, but it helps you get some rhythm, stay relaxed and time the pitcher. When he gets ready to release the ball, then you're ready to keep your hands back and start your stride. The pitcher can hold the ball as long as he wants as long as you have some movement and aren't choking your bat to death.

You can have the bat resting on your shoulder, which is comfortable for some, or you can have it down swinging low in front of you. As the pitcher's hand is coming forward, you should rotate back and then try to create bat speed to get to the ball.

GOOD COMFORT = GOOD TIMING = GOOD HITTING

As a player, you want to be as comfortable as you can be, both offensively and defensively. Successful players use different timing mechanisms to stay comfortable at the plate. For instance, some major-league players like to take a little hitch before they swing (which is not recommended for young players, but players at the major-league level are experienced enough, quick enough and strong enough to use the hitch as a timing mechanism), while others swing the bat loosely in front of them. Two players who used that method were George Brett and Mark McGwire.

George Brett

Loosely swinging the bat in front of you is a good device to use, because it is a very relaxed place to be. As you're swinging the bat in front of you, you're keeping your eyes on the pitcher, timing him. You can't get much more relaxed than that. As the pitcher starts to raise his leg, you bring the bat up to the ready position. You certainly don't have to worry about getting too tight with the bat in the cocked and ready position, because you bring it up at the last second. Your timing is exactly where you want it to be.

Good timing is key to good hitting. People who haven't faced a knuckleball pitcher sometimes wonder why those guys are so tough to hit. It's because they throw a hitter's timing completely off. That's why pitchers who seemingly don't throw hard but mix up the speeds of their pitches can play this game for a long time. Most hitters would definitely rather face a hard-throwing pitcher because hard throwers don't break timing—with those hitters it's just a matter of figuring out how to be quicker at the plate. But if that same hard thrower delivers a 98 mph fastball then comes back with an 85 mph change-up, the hitter's timing would be so far off that his bat might end up flying into the seats.

BE A SMART HITTER

Speaking of timing and pitchers, one way that you can combat a tough pitcher is to be a smart hitter. Being a smart hitter means knowing the game—knowing what pitches the pitcher is able to throw for strikes and what he likes to use in certain situations.

There are some basic rules of thumb for hitters when studying situations and counts. When I was playing, very few of our hitters were "allowed" to swing when the count was 3 and 0. Strong hitters' counts were 3 and 1 or 2 and 0. That's when we were allowed to center the pitch in one zone and look to do more than just hit a single. If the pitch was out of that area, we took it. Then on 3 and 2 we opened our personal zones a little bit, and if the pitch was close, we tried to simply put the ball in play. The mentality of managers changed over the years and they took the 3 and 1 count and made it a running count. That forces the hitter to treat the pitch more like a hit and run to protect the runner, instead of trying to center it and hit it out of the ballpark.

Unlike today's major league teams, when I was playing we didn't use a lot of video to learn the different pitchers, which might be similar to your team's approach. You can use the tool of conversation with your teammates before and during a game. For instance, our base stealers would sit together and try to pick apart the pitcher's weaknesses. Hitters sat together and watched how the pitcher worked in different situations. That's part of what makes the lead-off hitter important, because he acts as a "scout" for the other batters. His job is to force the pitcher to throw as many different types of pitches possible to see what is in his arsenal.

As you're watching the pitcher during the game, see what he does in certain situations, but also figure out what pitch or pitches he's having trouble getting over the plate for strikes. Then you can probably eliminate that pitch from your at-bat. We also used to concentrate on a pitcher throwing between innings. You can, too. Watch what he works on the most. If he keeps throwing the breaking ball in the dirt, you know you aren't going to get that on the first pitch.

Good pitchers still can throw off your timing by mixing up their pitches, but if you have an idea what's coming, you can be one step ahead.

MY TOUGHEST FUNDAMENTAL:

"When I first started working with Charley Lau in 1974, one of the most important fundamentals and hardest for me was extension through the ball, having a weight shift. ... I never had a weight shift or extension at the point of contact before that time (after 13 years of playing baseball). So, it was hard for me to grasp at first. But, through continuous hours of batting practice and hard work, I was able to do it and benefit from it. That was probably the most influential thing Charley ever taught me."

——*George Brett, my teammate during 1973-90, and a player who proved what can happen through hard work, dedication and skill*

RELAX THAT ELBOW!

One final note about the ready position. Young hitters (pre-high school) are often encouraged by their dads or coaches to keep their back elbow up in the ready position. That isn't a good idea because most young hitters don't know how to take their hands back and come down through the ball. The first tendency in a swing for kids who have their back elbow up is to drop their shoulder and back elbow, which gives them more of an upper cut. In fact, having the back elbow up forces kids to drop their back shoulder and get under the pitch. You have to be strong and disciplined to swing properly with your back elbow up.

Most players like to have a relaxed back elbow that will give them the fluid movement a hitter needs to coil back and then go forward with the pitch. A great example is former player Joe Morgan. If you remember watching Joe hit—or if you ever see a video of him hitting—you'll probably remember that he flapped his back elbow like he was trying to fly. Keeping your back elbow relaxed allows you to coil before going through your swing.

You want your elbows relaxed.

It is difficult to swing properly with your back elbow up.

As with so many other facets of baseball, quick hands in a swing are very important. Two good qualities to have are quick feet and quick hands, and your feet determine how quick your hands are going to be. Tied to the quick feet and hands in a swing is good hip rotation. All of those aspects acting quickly will help give you optimum power and bat speed through the swing.

The swing

WATCH THE CIRCLE

Besides being set up toward the back of the box to see the ball longer, you also want to see the ball as early as possible. The best way to do that is to watch the pitcher's release point. Pick an area—in your mind draw an imaginary circle—where the pitcher is going to release the ball. (You can determine that area by observing him while you're on deck.)

Younger players have a tendency to watch the pitcher's entire body during his motion, and the ball is the last thing they see. The best thing to do is to train yourself to look at the pitcher's normal release point and concentrate on that instead of watching all of the gyrations that he makes before he throws the ball.

Seeing the ball longer helps you decide whether or not to swing. The key is to recognize what you're swinging at. If you don't see it, don't swing. We like to tell our hitters that either you're going to swing fully, or you're not going to swing at all, rather than have a lot of check-swings, which show that you have poor recognition skills on that particular day.

CONTACT!

As the pitcher's arm is coming around for the delivery, you should start your motion back to load up for the swing as your eyes stay focused on the pitcher. When the pitcher's arm is moving forward you should start your stride, keeping your hands back, which allows you to recognize the type of pitch before you commit to your swing. If you don't keep your hands back and instead move your upper body forward, you won't be able to create an optimum bat speed, plus the pitch will seem faster to you. You want to stay back, let the ball come to you, and trust your quick hands to work when the ball gets to the plate. Try to hit with your hands and not with your body.

Keep your front shoulder in during your swing. The best way to do that is to stride directly toward the pitcher. When you stride toward the pitcher, your shoulder stays in, and you're able to maximize the bat's time in the hitting zone. If you stride "in the bucket," you open up your shoulder and the bat doesn't have as much time in the hitting zone, which decreases your chances of getting good wood (or aluminum) on the ball. Feel free to experiment to prove that point.

When you're taking your stride to swing, you need to step directly toward the target, the pitcher. Striding toward the target helps keep your hips free, and helps you stay balanced. One of two things will happen if you don't stride toward the target: 1.) You will stride across the box, which will lock your hips and make it difficult to swing through the pitch, or 2.) You will stride out ("in the bucket"), which will make it difficult for you to hit a pitch on the outside part of the plate. Ideally if you're going to swing, you want your bat head to be coming to the hitting zone when your foot hits the ground on your stride. Your stride should be short. Mine was about five or six inches.

You want to take a short stride and keep your hands back.

Going through your swing, you should try to hit the "inside" part of the ball. (If you try to hit the outside part of the ball, your arms are going to be extended too early, causing you to lose your balance with a long, looping swing.) By trying to hit the inside of the ball, you're going to have a short, compact swing, with a downward motion, which will help you stay above the ball. This type of swing, when properly executed, will help the ball carry farther.

You want to see the ball hit the bat. At the point of contact with the bat extended, as your head gets to the back shoulder from the front shoulder, your eyes should be looking directly down your arms to the bat hitting the ball.

Keep both hands on the bat through the swing. When you finish your swing, your top hand will automatically come off the bat. If you worry too much about keeping both hands on the bat at the end of your follow through, you may lose your balance and stumble if you miss the ball.

During your swing, you want to try to make contact with the ball in front of home plate, and then you want a good follow through.

DOWNWARD-TO-LEVEL SWING

As you swing, you want to swing through the ball and on top of the ball. In the introduction of this chapter, I mentioned the science and physics of hitting a baseball. A term that floats around regularly these days is to take a "downward-to-level" swing. That type of swing helps you stay on top of the ball, which gives you more line drives and will make the ball carry farther for you, but it also gives you the greatest physical chance to make contact. Consider if the ball is coming in straight (although, obviously, not all pitches are straight) and you take an uppercut, you have a small window of opportunity to make contact. But if you have a good downward-to-level swing on that same straight pitch, that window continues to stay open.

Common problems

Hitting is one of those areas where there are so many possible places to make a mistake to inhibit a fundamentally sound attack. Some players step in the bucket, some pull their heads, and some open up their front shoulder too soon, which pulls them off the ball. Many hitters have problems with plate coverage. You need to have good plate coverage to be a good hitter. The most common problems with young players seem to be hitching (lowering the bat before swinging), overstriding and stepping in the bucket (not striding toward the target).

Being able to make adjustments is important. Listening to what your coach tells you about flaws in your swing is key. Often players will continue to make the same mistakes until something drastic happens and they decide to get some help. Unfortunately in baseball, most times as a coach you have to let players first fail before you can help them.

THE HITCH

Most experienced hitting coaches will tell you that a hitch is fine if you end up in the hitting zone at the right time. Hitches only bother you if you're not in the hitting zone when the ball is there. If you're hitching when the ball is

in the zone, you'll have problems. To take out a hitch, basically you have to work it out on the batting tee and soft toss. As I mentioned earlier, some professional players use a hitch as a timing device, but I don't recommend that for an amateur.

You should not drop your hands, or hitch, before your swing.

OVERSTRIDING

Overstriding can hurt you, mainly for pitches on the outside part of the plate because you open up and you can't reach the ball. It is possible for a pitcher to throw inside and jam you with an overstride. The best solution is to use a batting tee or soft toss, and work on a short (about six inches) stride.

Your stride should be short, about six inches or so.

STEPPING IN THE BUCKET

Stepping in the bucket is the term used when, instead of striding toward the pitcher, you stride more toward third base (if you're a right-handed hitter) or first base (if you're a left-handed batter). The biggest problem with stepping in the bucket is that you end up too far from the plate to reach the pitch on the

outside corner. One possible solution is to take a definite step toward the target (the pitcher). If you do that consistently, the problem should work itself out.

A lot of times you'll see a player who steps in the bucket because he's afraid of the ball. Coaches may have suggested striding that way to open up hitters so they had two eyes on the ball when it came to the plate. Other hitting coaches have used stepping in the bucket for a player who has trouble getting his hips open during his swing. I never recommend that a hitter step in the bucket intentionally; however, some players feel that's the easiest way to get their hips open and contribute to the team.

Stride directly toward the pitcher and not "in the bucket."

UPPERCUT

One problem that hitters face—especially young hitters—is taking a long, looping uppercut instead of a good, compact, downward-to-level swing. Many players feel that in order to get the ball in the air, they need to drop their back shoulder and take a long, looping swing. The problem with this swing is that you actually cut down on the number of areas on the plate where you can hit the ball.

Most guys are only going to have a small area around their midsection where they can make contact with

You can have all sorts of problems when you uppercut (bottom left). Instead, you want a compact, downward-to-level swing.

an average fastball. With an uppercut you may not be able to make contact with an above-average fastball. One of the few exceptions to that rule is Mark McGwire, who had more of an uppercut in his swing. McGwire, however, was strong and quick enough that he still could hit the ball in front of the plate.

Ideally, you want to keep the bat on top of the ball, with the bat head above the ball hitting the inside of the ball. With that type of contact, you should create a backspin on the ball, which will make it carry. McGwire might be strong enough to use a long, looping swing to make the ball carry, but most players have to get it done a little differently.

DRIVE FOR SHOW (A.K.A. THE POWER HITTERS)

Like McGwire, many power hitters through the years have had an uppercut swing. Reggie Jackson had an up swing. Ted Williams had an up swing. Mickey Mantle, Harmon Killebrew and Babe Ruth all had upper cuts in their swings.

Mark McGwire

Today, Jim Edmonds and Jim Thome both swing with upper cuts. Barry Bonds has an uppercut swing, but his is very controlled. He chokes up on the bat, and he only takes an uppercut on pitches that are down and inside. However, he also has the ability to stay on top of the ball that's higher in the strike zone, and drive it to center field. Juan Gonzalez is the same type of hitter.

In fact, the uppercut swing comes into play for most power hitters on balls that are low and in. If the player is strong enough to power the ball out of the park, that's fine. Most hitters aren't strong enough and quick enough to do that. All good hitters, though, have the ability to take a downward-to-level stroke on balls that are out over the plate, and drive balls to the outfield. Great examples of guys who consistently stay on top of the ball for power include Albert Pujols and Manny Ramirez.

DO AS I SAY, NOT AS I DO

One thing that kids have done for years is to try to emulate their favorite player. A lot of kids today try to copy Nomar Garciaparra's pre-hit ritual of playing with his batting gloves, and then tapping his toes in the box. That is Nomar's way of getting ready to hit. Each major-league player has his own quirks to help him stay comfortable and his own way of swinging the bat. As a youngster coming up, you should concentrate on learning the basic ways to hit and play defense. Then as you get older and better in the game, you can develop your own hitting style and fielding style to help you stay relaxed and get the most out of your abilities.

Jim Thome

MY BEST ADVICE:

"Stay within yourself. Don't try to be a player that you're not. Just because Barry Bonds goes out and hits 70 home runs, don't try to go out and hit 70. You don't have the power that he does. Just do what you're capable of doing."
——*George Brett, Hall of Famer and career .305 hitter*

Tools

There are several time-tested hitting tools that help players work on their skills or work through various hitting mechanic flaws. One of the best devices is a batting tee. On a daily basis during the season, players who want to improve their batting hit off the tee. They do a lot of tee work.

The batting tee helps you develop a swing to stay on top of the ball and hit inside of the ball. Overall, the tee is a great tool because you can adjust the height, you can move the ball in or out, and you can move it toward the front or back of the plate to work on different pitch locations. It's a super tool.

Another drill to improve your swing is soft toss, which is when a coach sits on a bucket in the opposite batter's box, and just tosses the ball underhand to let the hitter swing at it. At the same time, the coach watches the hitter's mechanics, making sure he is swinging properly. Soft toss is a good drill to use to help develop quick hands, to pop the bat through the hitting zone.

Pepper also is a great drill. In pepper, there is one player with a bat and two or three players about 12 feet away, softly throwing the ball, while the batter tries to work on bat control, hitting the ball from one fielder to the next. Pepper is a great drill before a game if it rains and you can't take batting practice. Pepper is an easy drill for you to use during your pregame warm ups.

One of the best ways to work on your hitting skills is by batting off a pitching machine or having a coach come throw the ball to you. Today, teams often go to an indoor batting cage before a game. At the major-league level, a lot of teams have batting cages under their stadiums where players can take extra swings. It's great to take BP like that on the day of a game, but it's especially beneficial on non-game days when the number of swings you take isn't dictated by a game time.

All of those tools and drills are useful to every hitter and should help you improve your overall swing.

Getting hit by a pitch

In case this hasn't happened to you yet, or no one has explained this to you, then I hate to be the bearer of bad news, but there is something you need to learn. As a hitter you need to understand that inevitably, at some point in your baseball career, you WILL be hit by a pitch. However, there are certain movements you can make at the plate to lessen your chance of serious injury.

How often a player gets hit depends on the individual. I think getting hit by a pitch goes back to pitch recognition, knowing where you are in

Frank White

relation to home plate, and your athletic ability. Some players can have a stance close to the plate, and they barely move if the pitch is high and a few inches from their bodies. Other players can have the ball closer and nonchalantly lean back to avoid getting hit. Those players are familiar with pitch recognition and their place in the box. Some players might not be that "comfortable" on an inside pitch. (Keep in mind, most hitters aren't completely comfortable when a pitch is high and tight.)

Regardless of your comfort level, when the ball is coming toward your midsection—your ribs—you have to decide what you're going to do to get out of the way or lessen the blow of the ball. If you raise up your arms in that situation, the ball will probably hit you in the midsection and could very easily crack or break some ribs. As soon as you recognize that the ball is headed toward your upper body, you need to turn in (away from the pitcher) so the ball can hit you somewhere in the back. If you're quick enough, and the ball is a little more behind you, you can hit the deck and let the pitch go by. I'll caution you on this, however, because if you're not quick enough, the ball could hit you in the head and hurt more than it would if it hit you in the ribs.

This is a no-no (left). I've seen many players injure their ribs when they don't know how to get hit by a pitch. Ideally, you want to turn your head and roll away from the pitch (right).

ALWAYS REMEMBER
TO TURN YOUR HEAD AWAY FROM THE BALL!

If the pitch is coming toward your head, unless it's a slow curveball that you can duck to avoid, you need to roll away so the back of your helmet is the only part of your head exposed to the ball.

When the pitch is around your waist, you can bend over, pushing back your hips.

On an inside pitch that is below your midsection, there are three ways to avoid getting hit. Depending on how low the pitch is coming, you can turn in your legs, bend over to where your hips push back, scoot your feet back, or turn your head and shoulder away from the pitch. Again, it goes back to pitch recognition and your athletic ability.

IT WILL HURT

The first thing to do with children—especially if they're afraid of being hit by a pitch—is to let them know that if they get hit by a ball, it will probably hurt. Period. A lot of times dads, brothers, uncles or coaches will get a little macho and tell a child that the ball won't hurt. "Don't be a sissy." I'm here to tell you that the ball does hurt. I think if we tell kids that fact at an early age, when they do get hit and it does hurt, they might cry, but the pain won't make them quit playing baseball.

On the other hand, if you tell them that it's not going to hurt, and you build up their confidence, then they get whacked—on the elbow especially—and it hurts, they're going to wonder why you lied to them about it. That may cause you to lose the kid forever from playing this great game. This applies to other aspects of the game. Defensively, a ball could take a bad hop and hit them; or they could misjudge a fly ball and get hit. And, yes, in each of those instances the ball can hurt.

If you want to work with a child on getting out of the way of pitches, first take a crew sock and roll it up into a ball. Then put him in his batting stance and tell him that you're going to throw inside. Let him work on rolling away from the ball. If the sock hits him, it shouldn't hurt.

The best way to get used to turning away is to watch the ball all the way into the catcher's mitt on any pitch that you're not swinging at. That helps you develop the ability to roll away, and it also helps you recognize the ball's location on the plate. Besides experimenting with your swing and stance, the batting cage is a good place to simply stand there and learn to watch the ball go to the catcher.

Hitting off-speed pitches

For me, learning to hit the off-speed pitch was a matter of seeing it enough times. When you don't see enough of them, you get startled when you do see a change-up, curve ball, etc. At our level, we know the pitchers and we know what pitches they throw. We know what they are more apt to throw with two strikes versus one strike. When you have gained general knowledge of who's pitching, then you can make your own adjustments.

Learning to hit the change-up and curve ball is just a matter of recognizing them and letting your eyes get used to seeing those pitches. As you see them on a regular basis, you can more easily distinguish between a fastball and a curve ball. Then once you see a curve ball on the way, you can realize that if it starts above your letters then it's going to be a strike, but if it starts at your waist it's going to be a ball, so you try to lay off it.

The main way to improve your off-speed hitting is by simply working on it. Having someone throw you fastballs and then change ups and curve balls is beneficial. You want to keep your hands back on off-speed pitches. Now you see the importance of having quick hands. A guy who takes a short stride, recognizes the fastball and the off-speed pitch, is still able to use his hands. You have to be able to stride out but keep your hands back and recognize, "Oops, not a fastball but hold it, hold it, POW there it goes." To the hitter's advantage, some pitchers, even at the professional level, tip their hand—so to speak—when they're throwing a pitch other than the fastball. In the windup many times, they'll raise their hands higher on a breaking ball than on a fastball. You should look for things like that from the bench to help you and your teammates out as much as possible.

Hitting in the clutch

Being able to hit in the clutch often takes ice in your veins. A lot of times the game is on the line and you're the man, so you have to be able to tune people out and concentrate on the task at hand. Nearly every hitter will at some time be at the plate in a clutch situation—everyday players and bench players.

MY BEST ADVICE:

"Try to hit the ball hard, not far. When you try to hit the ball far, you get a lot of tension in your hands and in your legs. You also start jumping at the ball when you start swinging too hard. The harder you swing and the more tension you have, the more body parts move around and get out of sync. If you can control your swing, be short and quick and through the ball, you'll be more consistent. We tell the major leaguers that when they're struggling."
—*George Brett, Hall of Fame third baseman, and my teammate during 1973-90*

Hitters have to remember that when the bases are loaded, or you have a first-and-second or second-and-third situation, the pressure is on the pitcher. You just have to be selective in what you want to try to hit because the pitcher has to throw a strike. As a hitter, you have to make sure the pitch is what you're looking for at that particular time.

George Brett was a very good clutch hitter. I'd like to think that I was a pretty good clutch hitter. Hal McRae was excellent. Today you can look at Manny Ramirez and Juan Gonzalez. There are a lot of players like them in the major leagues today who can flat-out hit, regardless of the game situation.

WHITE'S WORDS OF WISDOM

- Always keep your eye on the ball. Try to see the ball with both eyes.
- Always step toward the target.
- Always try to keep your weight on the back leg and swing down through the ball.
- Don't open your shoulder too soon because it pulls you off the ball.

Bunting

Bunting is crucial to fundamental baseball. I think everyone on the team should know how to bunt. Baseball always comes down to knowing the fundamental skills of bunting—who can do it, who can't do it, how bad we need it, but we can't do it because the current batter doesn't have confidence in his ability to lay it down. The mastery of bunting is one of the best ways to keep yourself in the ballgame because you always have the ability to advance the runners into scoring position.

Early in my career, I bunted a lot. In fact, I held the Royals' team record for sacrifice bunts in a season at 18, until Johnny Damon broke it. I used to try to get about 10 drag or push bunt base hits a year, trying to keep my head above water. You could say I was a bunting machine.

Some players like to bunt when they're in a hitting slump. Laying a bunt down really doesn't help you get out of a slump, but it keeps your head above water until you can figure out what is wrong with your swing. However, if your hitting problem is that you're not seeing the ball, bunting can help with that, because when you bunt, you force yourself to concentrate more on seeing the ball hit the bat.

STRATEGIES FOR BUNTING

1. Bunting for a base hit is supposed to be a surprise. When you're bunting for a base hit, the ball should be barely fair or foul. You don't want to allow an easy play for the pitcher or any other infielder.
2. When you're bunting for a sacrifice, you want to get the ball out on the grass three or four feet to give the runner an opportunity to get to the next base.
3. Push bunting is when you place the ball in between first base and the pitcher's mound. The goal is to get the first baseman to commit over and then get into a foot race between you and the pitcher.

FUNDAMENTAL BUNTING TECHNIQUES

The biggest problem in bunting is the hitter's approach. Many players don't know what they're trying to do by bunting. When you are asked to bunt, you need to know your goal for that at-bat, but you also need to understand that bunting is a vital component in the game of baseball. Even if you feel that the pitch is one that you could hit hard, if the coach gives you the bunt sign, there is a reason. Successful teams have players who know how to bunt and are willing to do so when needed.

Figure 3-18

If you're going to drag bunt for a base hit, you have to make sure that your feet are in fair territory. If your normal stance has you at the back of the box, when you position yourself for a drag bunt, your back foot is actually in foul territory. You have to move up in the box. As the pitch is on its way, drop your right foot back—if you're a right-handed hitter—and point the head of your bat at the first base bag in order to get the ball to go down the third base line (Figure 3-18). Immediately upon making contact, you're off and running.

The sacrifice bunt isn't as deceptive as the drag bunt because it isn't a surprise. Even though a lot of people know when you're going to sacrifice, you don't want to turn around too soon. The first thing you do when you sacrifice is tell yourself that you're going to be out. Then you want to stand there and make sure you get the bunt down before you start running.

For the squeeze bunt, you must wait until the last minute before you display it. If you give it away too soon, the pitcher is going to throw the ball up and try to knock you down to clear the way for the catcher to tag the runner coming down from third. Or if the runner hasn't completely committed to coming home, you getting brushed back gives the catcher a clear vision for a pick-off attempt at third. The base runner at third takes his lead, then when the pitcher's front foot strikes the ground, the runner breaks for home. Once that front foot hits the ground, the pitcher can't change his arm angle. As soon as that lead foot strikes the ground, the runner is going home as hard as he can go, and then it's up to the batter to turn around at the last minute and put the ball in play.

Some teams use what we call a "slash" bunt. This is a technique that really isn't used much until at least high school—and even then it's not common to see. In the simplest terms, a slash

You should have your body squared toward the pitcher and make sure you get the bunt down on a sacrifice.

bunt is when the batter shows bunt, but pulls it back and swings away. We tell the hitter in a "slash" situation that if he sees the shortstop leave early to cover third base, then he should take the bat back and just try to hit a hard ground ball through the hole at shortstop, because there will be a big hole open. The slash would be the offense's way to defend the infielders trying to anticipate the bunt.

WATCH YOUR ANGLE

Regardless of which type of bunt you're attempting, a key to keep in mind is the bat angle. The head of the bat has to be above the ball. You can't flinch or "throw" the bat at the ball except on a squeeze bunt. Your arms need to be flexed out in front of your body, with your knees bent, and you need to have plate coverage. In essence, you want to "catch" the ball with the bat. If the pitch is low, bend your knees, keeping your bat head up. You

Your bat head should be at an angle, and you want to make sure to not wrap your top hand around the bat. Also, you should have some bend in your knees.

don't want to drop the bat head to go for a low pitch. That only leads to pop-ups. I like to start low, with my knees bent, and then come up, because it is hard to be straight up and have to go straight down to bunt a low pitch.

WHITE'S WORDS OF WISDOM

- Always make sure you're in fair territory when you square around to bunt. That will give you a better chance of being in fair territory when you lay the ball down.
- Always make sure your knees are bent, your head is up, your hands are out front, and the bat head is above the ball.
- Always point the bat head toward the first base line if you want the ball to go to third. If you're left-handed, point the bat toward the third base line to send the ball down the first base line.
- Don't square around too soon.
- Don't square around facing the pitcher, because if the ball is inside you won't be able to get out of the way. You also don't have as much plate coverage when you square around and face the pitcher.

Chapter 4

Running for Gold

Aside from pitching and defense, more games are won and lost through base running than any other facet of baseball. You don't have to be a fast runner to be a good base runner; you just have to be an alert runner. For example, let's say you hit a ball in the alley, you make a good turn around first and the outfielder bobbles the ball, then you hustle to second base. That's a good base runner. That example doesn't take speed, it just takes a player who is alert, gets around first base, and watches and takes off for second base when he sees the outfielder's inconsistency in fielding the ball. You can be the slowest player on your team but still be one of your team's best base runners.

I have witnessed some great base runners during my career. The first one that comes to mind is Rickey Henderson. He was the best. He had strong legs, a strong body, great acceleration, and he stayed low. He was simply a tremendous base runner. Amos Otis, Willie Wilson, Vince Coleman and Otis Nixon were all not only fast base runners, but good base runners. George Brett and Hal McRae were good base runners.

Our Royals teams took pride in solid base running. In 1977 we had seven guys steal at least 20 bases. When we hit a ball to the outfield we were looking for a double, trying to put pressure on the outfielders. We took pride on making good turns, stealing bases, scoring—getting good leads off second base to score on a single. We tried to take aggressiveness to the next level. I think our team had some of the best base run-

Rickey Henderson

AP/WWP

ners in the game during the 1970s and '80s. I'm convinced that good, aggressive base running was a large key to our success.

THE IDEAL BASE RUNNER

The first quality that all good base runners possess is instinct. They try to create as much confusion for the pitcher as they can. Good base runners are also adept at stealing the catcher's signs from second base and relaying the pitch or the location to the hitter. They are adept at going from first to third on base hits to the outfield. Keen runners take an extra base by reading the angles of the outfielders and the direction they're going, and know how difficult a throw it may be for the outfielder based on that observation. Good runners are able to get a good jump off third on the contact play—contact means as soon as the ball is hit, you're off and running, trying to score.

Good running technique is very important. When I was in the Royals' Baseball Academy, they brought in Wes Santee, the great miler from the University of Kansas, to teach us running form—how to incorporate our elbows into our running, and how to get more power in our running. Young kids today, with the popularity of soccer and basketball, and other sports, learn those running techniques pretty early in life. In football you learn a natural running technique, especially if you're one of the players carrying the ball. Running technique in baseball is sometimes more important than running speed because the technique—making good turns around the bases or tracking down a ball in the outfield—gets you there just as fast as the player with good speed.

I like to see aggressive base runners, guys who take a primary lead at a base, and then take an aggressive secondary lead and are ready to run if the pitch is in the dirt. Aggressive runners are ready to go if the ball is hit, or ready to get back to the bag if the hitter takes a pitch. I love to see players be alert to everything that is happening on the field as it applies to base running.

Stance and start

LEADING OFF

The length of a player's lead off of first base depends on the player. When you look at the Lou Brocks, Rickey Hendersons and Willie Wilsons of baseball, their lead was usually somewhere between 13 and 14 feet off the bag. Two of these players are in the record books for steals. They were smart and fast. Most players should operate somewhere between eight and 13 feet off the bag. That usually translates to taking two steps away from the base, and then a couple shuffles.

This is a good, "safe" lead from first.

At second base, you're looking at a little bigger lead. Your initial lead will be 15 to 18 feet, then a good secondary lead, which means a couple good shuffles on the pitch. Base stealers may get 20 to 22 feet away from the bag at second.

When you're taking your lead off a base—regardless of the base—you should have your knees bent in a good athletic position, about shoulder-width apart. You want to be as relaxed as possible. At the same time, you want to have your arms in a relaxed "power" position, close to your body. You don't want them hanging down in front of you. Your lead foot should be open slightly to help get your hips open in a running situation, whether that is a steal or advancing on a hit. If your front foot is not open, you'll usually force your body to come up when you take your cross-over step, which translates into lost time.

KEEP YOUR EYES ON THE PITCHER

When taking your lead off the base, you have to know all of the rules that go along with the left-hander coming to first base versus the right-hander coming to first base. You need to know that the right-handed pitcher has to step off the rubber to throw to first.

As a base runner—especially with thoughts of stealing—you should always pay attention to certain moves the pitcher will make when he's throwing home. There are a lot of movements that you can pick from a pitcher. For instance, sometimes when pitchers are going home from the stretch their legs are closer than when they are coming to first.

On a right-handed pitcher, watch his right heel. If his right heel comes up, then you know he's either stepping off the rubber or throwing over to first base. Some right-handers might have a little bend, a little flex, in their right knee before they go to the plate. They might also make a different movement in their hips, shoulders or head.

There are many little things that you look for in a left-hander. Most left-handers look at first and go home or they look home and come to first. Watch their glove placement. Sometimes they raise their glove higher before they come to first, and hold it lower when they go to the plate. They also may have a shoulder lean or a different rock in their movement.

Pitchers even have a tendency to give the hitter an idea of the next pitch. A lot of times in their motion, pitchers will raise their hand higher on a curve ball than they will on a fast ball, or vice versa. There are many things that you can try to pick apart by watching the pitcher. You have to pay attention and learn from watching. Little things that pitchers do often let you, as a base runner—or a hitter—know what they're going to do. The key is to gather the information and know how to use it.

MY TOUGHEST FUNDAMENTAL

"Reading pitchers—pick-off moves, studying time to home plate, seeing if a pitcher is going to tip-off whether he's throwing home or to the base— was a difficult base running fundamental for me."
—*Roberto Alomar, who is ranked in the top 10 for active career runs scored leaders*

Doug Pensinger/Getty Images

Roberto Alomar

Stealing second

THE SWIPE

Stealing a base at the little-league level usually isn't as difficult as it is when players get older, because a young catcher doesn't have the accuracy or arm strength to throw out a lot of runners. Still, you should always work on good base-stealing techniques. The first thing to recognize as a base stealer is how far off the base you can get and still be comfortable. At a younger age your length off the base isn't as important, because the pitcher usually isn't very quick on his delivery to the plate.

For the purpose of the book, we'll mainly talk about stealing second base (going from first to second), since that is the most common stealing situation. I like to have non-base stealers—players who aren't as likely to run—about eight to 10 feet off the bag. Base stealers should be in the neighborhood of 12 to 13 feet off the bag. Runners need to know such things as a pitcher's move to first and how he varies his moves to first. Also, when the pitcher does throw over, the runner needs to know if that was his best move. That's where the first base coach comes into play. The coach should be able to tell the runner if he just saw the pitcher's best move, or if the runner can move off a little more.

Once the pitcher is in his stretch position and you have taken your lead, you want to focus on one area of his body. When you're on first base, and a right-handed pitcher is on the mound, you want to focus on his right heel. If the heel stays down, he's throwing to the plate. If his heel comes up, he's throwing to first base. Some pitchers like to make all sorts of upper-body fakes, but his heel is the indicator. If you focus on his whole body you might fall for one of those fakes and either get a bad jump—if you're stealing—or want to camp out too close to the bag.

While you're leading off, most of your body's weight should be from the middle of your body toward your left side. With that type of weight balance, if the pitcher throws to first, your weight is already leaning that way; and if he throws home, you're in a good power position to get a good jump.

When you take off for second, you want to drive the left side of your body across and toward second base, keeping your body low through the initial

I liked to take a quick jab step with my right foot when I stole because it gave me a quick start.

strides—until about the fourth or fifth stride—then you'll start to rise up. (Even though you don't want to count while you're stealing in a game situation, you're looking at about 13 strides and then the slide into second base.)

Your initial stride will depend on your speed and athletic ability. Some guys can effectively use a cross-over step, where their first stride is left over right. Other guys will take a quick jab step with their right foot to help get their momentum going. That's the move I used because it opened my hips and allowed me to stay low.

MY BEST ADVICE

"Remember that the first step when stealing a base is the most important step you'll take. Then once you get going, stay low to the ground to keep up your speed."
—*Roberto Alomar, who is ranked in the top five for active career stolen base leaders*

As you're running toward second base, a good practice is to take a quick glance toward home plate to know what's happening with the ball. Many coaches will tell their hitter to not swing when the steal sign is on, but you should still look in. The "old-timers" say that you shouldn't glance back because it takes away from your speed, but what happens if the batter ropes a low line drive? You run the risk of being nailed or doubled off the base, or being confused when you don't know where the ball is. Runners get into trouble when they take a long look and slow down their running in the process. When I say glance, I mean glance. Keep up your running speed but just glance quickly enough that you know what's happening with the pitch.

By taking a quick glance you also avoid getting faked by the middle infielders covering the bag. One such situation that comes to my mind happened in the 1987 World Series between the Minnesota Twins and the St. Louis Cardinals. Lonnie Smith was stealing for the Cardinals, and the hitter belted the pitch to deep left field. Lonnie didn't glance back to see the ball, and the middle infielder covering second acted like a throw was coming from the catcher, so Lonnie slid into the base. Well, the ball was caught by the left fielder and the Twins were able to double off Lonnie at first because he didn't have time to recover from his slide. That's a great example of why looking in is important.

TAKING ADVANTAGE OF BALLS IN THE DIRT

Watch for the ball that bounces in the dirt in front of the catcher. You should try to learn how to read the angle of the ball as it enters the hitting area. If you anticipate the pitch being in the dirt, as soon as the ball hits the ground, take off for second base because the catcher very rarely fields that ball cleanly, even in the major leagues. The percentage is high enough in favor of the runner that the ball in the dirt is an aggressive way to advance into scoring position.

Infield grounder

RUN IT OUT!

Once the ball is hit on the ground, out of instinct the batter usually watches to see where the ball is headed. However, once he starts down the base line he should be running as hard as he can. As a batter running toward first base, you should incorporate your elbows as much as possible to help with your running power. Run in a straight line and go "through" the bag—in other words don't slow down when you get to the bag. As you get close, aim for the front part of the base, not the middle of the bag (Figure 4-4).

Figure 4-4

During a game at Kansas City early in the 2001 season, on a night when it was damp, Jose Guillen of the Tampa Bay Devil Rays hit the top of the bag, his foot slipped across and his heel caught on the other side. He injured his knee. Always aim for the hardest part of the base, which is the front, to be quickest and less prone to injury.

We often see players take a long leap on their last stride to first, and some dive to the bag. When you take a long leap, not only do you lose some valuable speed, but you also risk possible injury. For instance, if you come up short and your heel hits the ground first, you can hyperextend your knee, or injure your Achilles tendon.

I don't recommend diving headfirst into first base either, because you risk injury to your head, neck, shoulders and arms if you go into the base improperly or if the first baseman has to move to catch the incoming throw. Kenny Lofton, whom I consider a great base runner, incidentally, injured his shoulder diving into first and had to have shoulder surgery. Some runners and coaches feel that if you dive into the bag that you're going to touch the base faster. That's really not the case. In fact, in a lot of instances you're going to be a little slower.

Breaking up the double play

HIT THE GROUND RUNNING—ON A GROUNDER

A mark of a good base runner is that he knows his responsibility when the ball is hit on the ground. Just because you, as a runner from first, get thrown out at second on a ground ball doesn't mean that you can't try to help your team. Or just because there are two outs and a grounder is hit toward third base, you, as a runner on first, aren't automatically out at second. There are two rules of thumb that apply to a runner on first base when the ball is hit on the ground: 1.) Break up the double play with less than two outs, and 2.) Try to beat the throw to second with two outs. Always work to get a good jump and read the ball off the bat so that you will know which you need to do.

The first rule applies when there are less than two outs. When you first reach base with less than two outs, pay attention to the middle infielders, the pitcher and the first baseman. The pitcher always looks back at the shortstop and second baseman to see which one is going to cover the bag if the ball is hit back to the mound. That gives you an advantage. A lot of times the first baseman will look at one of the middle infielders and let him know which one he's throwing to if the ball is grounded to him.

As the pitcher goes into his motion, you want to get a good secondary lead and then if the ball is hit on the ground, get down to second base as hard as you can and try to break up a double play. Your objective in breaking up a double play is to slide into the defensive player covering the base, forcing him to not make a throw to first or to make a bad throw to first, thereby helping extend your team's trip to the plate. As you're running toward second, you need to figure out on which side of the bag the second baseman or the shortstop—whichever is taking the throw—is going to be. Once you know where the defensive player is taking the throw, your goal is to be on that side of the bag with your plan of action to break up the double play. Baseball's rule, considered the "McRae Rule," named after one of my former teammates, Hal McRae, says that you have to start your slide before you get to the bag, and if you slide away from the bag, you have to be able to reach it with your hand.

In terms of today's major-league players breaking up double plays, there aren't many players who stand out as aggressive runners into second. Mike Sweeney does an excellent job. I like the way he's approached it, because he likes to get down to second as hard as he can and do the best job he can to break it up. Roberto Alomar does a good job of trying to break it up. Overall in the league, though, we don't see it happening as much as we used to—or as much as we should see it.

There are a lot of players who come to mind from when I played. Obviously McRae was good. Brett did a good job. Don Baylor, Frank Robinson, Kirk Gibson and Brian Downing, among several others, were very aggressive—to put it mildly—coming into second base. Believe me, I can remember those guys. In the "old" days, we didn't have rules regarding how we could slide or how we couldn't take players out. The "McRae Rule" is one reason that runners aren't as aggressive today at breaking up double plays. There is a chance that your league or team has a rule regarding how you can go into second base, so be aware of that.

The second rule of thumb when there is a ground ball to the infield, applies to when you're on first with two outs. In that situation, you should center your mind on beating the ball to second base. Have in your mind that the ball is going to be a grounder to deep short, so you will run in a straight line to the base. If the ball happens to go to the outfield, you can make the adjustment for your turn and head for third base. Still, your primary objective as a runner at first with two outs is to beat the throw to second.

RULES FOR OTHER BASE RUNNERS ON A GROUND BALL

As a runner on second or third when a ball is grounded or lined in the infield, you have to make a quick decision depending on the situation. The general rule says that if you're on second with less than two outs and the ball is grounded to the third-base side of second, make sure you don't get thrown out at third base. With that in mind, pay attention to the positioning of the short-stop. If the shortstop is to your right side—over your right shoulder—and the ball is grounded to your right, then you need to stay put. If the ball is grounded up the middle and gets past the pitcher, then you should try to advance.

If there are runners on second and third with less than two outs and the hitter grounds it in the infield, the call to run or not is generally made by the third base coach or the manager. As a runner at second, you mainly need to know if the runner on third is running home. As elementary as this may sound, if the runner on third is not running, then the runner on second needs to know that so he can stay put. If that runner on third is going—or if there is no runner on third—and the ball is grounded to the right side of the infield, you can usually advance to third base.

Fly ball to the outfield

Any time you're on base and a ball is flied to the outfield, you want to be looking for ways to advance to the next base. Therefore, fundamentally, you need to know how to tag up. The first thing to keep in mind when tagging up on a fly ball to the outfield is to know when to leave the base. Ideally, as an aggressive base runner you're anticipating the catch being made.

As the outfielder is getting in position to make the catch, you want to be in a good running stance with one foot on the bag and the other foot facing the next base. You always need to face the outfielder who is catching the ball. In other words, you want to get in position on the base so that your feet are aimed toward the next base, but you can still see the fielder catch the ball.

Figure 4-3   Figure 4-4

For instance, if you're on second base and the ball is hit to right field, you want your left foot on the bag and your right foot facing third base so you can see when to take off (Figure 4-3). If your right foot is on the bag in that situation, you have to look over your shoulder to watch the right fielder, which could cost you some time. Or if you're on second and the ball is hit to deep left, you want your right foot on the bag and your left foot facing third (Figure 4-4). Then if you know the ball is deep enough for you to tag, as soon as the outfielder makes the catch, you're running as hard as you can to the next base.

Most of the time you're going to be tagging up from second base or third base. There are a few instances when a runner at first will tag up, but generally he is looking for other situations to advance to second base on a fly ball. For instance, I tell base runners at first that if the ball is hit deep to left-center or right-center, where the outfielder is in full sprint to reach the ball, then go ahead and run toward second—and maybe even a few steps around the base. If the ball falls, you should be able to reach third and possibly try to score. If the outfielder catches the ball, you have enough time to retrace your steps and hustle back to first base.

With runners on first and third—or second and third—on a routine fly ball, the trail runner jogs away from the bag slowly and watches the play. At the same time, the runner on third is tagging up. If the outfielder's throw is high and goes all the way to home plate, then the runner at first or second should run to the next base. If it's a low throw, he stays put because the defense will probably cut off the ball and throw to second.

Extra bases

MAKING THE TURNS

If you know you have a base hit—you know the ball is out of the infield—you want to start making your turn around first early with the plan to go to second if the outfielder makes a mistake. Between home plate and first base on most fields, there is a chalked box that comes out from the "normal" baseline, the 45-foot box. On a base hit, the corner of that box is the perfect place to start making your turn to round first base. You don't want to go straight down the line, then try to make your turn after hitting first base. You basically want to start your turn at a 45-degree angle at the start of that box.

The turns you make around the bases that enable you to get to the next base faster are what make you stand out as a good base runner. Making good turns and keeping your head up and your ears open will help you become a good base runner. (see page 96)

Running on base hits

Seeing your team run itself out of a possible rally because of bad base running is just as frustrating as anything else in baseball, especially if your team has trouble scoring runs. A main rule of thumb in base running is to never make the first or last out of an inning at third base.

MAKING
THE TURNS

These are the angles you should take from home toward second when you know you have at least a potential double. To show where you want to break, we have placed a baseball at the start of the 45-foot box.

Nevertheless, to be an aggressive base runner means that you're always looking to advance at least two bases whenever possible. So if you're on first base and the ball is hit between center field and the right-field line, you're making a good turn around second with the plan that you will reach third base. When you're on second base and the ball is hit to the outfield, you're making a good turn around third with the plan to score. With these rules in mind, running from first you should only have to worry about picking up your third-base coach on balls that are hit to right field, because the other balls are in front of you and you can decide what you need to do. And, running from second base you should pay attention to what that coach is telling you to do.

As an aggressive runner you should watch the outfielder's angle toward the ball to determine whether or not you're going to run to third base from first. If, for example, the ball is hit toward the gap in left-center, and the center fielder is charging hard for it, you can probably advance to third because it's going to be tough for him to get the ball, stop, and make a strong throw to get you. Other good situations for a runner are when the center fielder is charging hard on a ball to his left or if he is going to his right and has to backhand the ball.

One word of caution, though. Whatever you do, if the ball is a line drive with less than two outs, make sure it reaches the outfield. One of baseball's most frustrating plays for a base runner (and a hitter) is to get doubled off on a liner to the infield. Let's say you're on base and the batter drives a sharp line drive at the second baseman or the shortstop, and you get caught too far from the base. You will probably get doubled off. The rule of thumb on any line drive hit head high or lower, you freeze, wait for the ball to clear the infield, and then proceed to the next base if it's safe. Many players don't pay attention to that particular part of the game when they are on base. Even though their coach warns them to be aware of the line drives and tries to keep them alert, they still get doubled off.

The reason those players get thrown out at a base is because as soon as the ball is hit they take two to three strides without thinking. If the ball is a line drive to one of the infielders, the runner doesn't have an opportunity to get back to the bag. The only place where you don't have much of a choice is if you're on first and the ball is a line drive to the first baseman. That's the most difficult play to avoid getting doubled off. You need to always be aware of game situations.

MAKING AN EXCHANGE

There are times when a team that is up by a run or two might exchange an out for a run. That is, if you've got a slow runner on second base, and the batter singles to the outfield, the coach might let the batter go for second in an attempt to force the cut-off guy to stop the ball, enabling the slow runner to score. That's a way to "steal" a run in exchange for the batter-runner possibly being thrown out at second. That's not really bad base running. In that case it is smart, aggressive base running.

If you've got guys on first and second with the slower runner on second, tell your runner on first that if the ball goes through the infield on the ground, he probably doesn't have to help the lead runner. In that case you're probably OK to try to score. However, if the ball is a line drive to the outfield, and the third-base coach continues to send the runner, the faster guy should try to get into the eyesight of the cut-off man and force him to make a decision to either let the ball go home or cut it off and go for the third out. By then, the slower runner has already crossed the plate, and exchanged the out for the run. If the game is tied or your team is down by a run, you probably don't try that. But when you are up by a run or two and you're trying to increase your lead, then you try to put pressure on the defense and force them to make some tough decisions at tough times. If you can steal a run from it, then that run is more valuable than the out at that particular time.

Those plays also highlight the importance of runners paying attention to their first and third base coaches.

"Hot box"

A game that a lot of kids like to play is known as "hot box" or "pickle." (Technically it's called a rundown.) As a game, this is where you have one man running between two bases, while two guys playing catch try to get the runner out. As a kid it's fun trying to see what different moves you can make in an attempt to reach the other base safely. I had a lot of fun playing the game as a kid. If we were quick we could get out of it quite often because we didn't know anything about going out of the baseline. So, when the guy with the ball got close, we could fake him out and go wide to get around him. Even though the quickness and moves that I developed before reaching the major leagues came from playing football and dodgeball in school, "hot box" is an invaluable way to hone your skills.

The main thing for a runner to keep in mind in a game situation is to control the first sense of panic that sets in when you get in a rundown. Don't panic.

If you get caught in a rundown when there are no other runners on base, the key is to simply keep distance between you and the defensive player with the ball, and don't commit to a base until they make you commit. When more than two defensive players are involved in the rundown, some runners will try to run into the guy who released the ball in hopes of getting some type of interference or obstruction call if that extra defensive man doesn't clear the area quickly enough. That's a nice strategy, but don't necessarily try it for the first time during your league championship game.

If there is a runner on third base and a grounder goes to first or third, and there is a throw to the plate that forces a rundown, that runner's responsibility is to stay in the "hot box" as long as he can while the batter-runner advances to second base.

Along those same lines, if there are runners at second and third and the lead runner gets in a rundown, the runner from second should go ahead and move to third base, then hope the lead runner is able to score, while the batter-runner heads for second base. That way, if the lead runner gets thrown out, his team still has two men in scoring position.

Sliding

There are four basic types of slides used today: headfirst, straight-in, pop-up and hook. Obviously, the game situation and the base where you're headed will determine which slide you use.

The straight-in slide is one that you're using when you're "simply" trying to be safe. For instance, if you're going for a double on a ball hit down the left-field line that the left fielder cuts off, then the straight-in slide is definitely a good slide to use. Earlier in the chapter I talked about going from first to second on an infield grounder with two outs. That's another situation where you want to use the straight-in slide, assuming the ball doesn't go through to the outfield.

You want to keep a little bend in your right knee, lean your body back slightly and keep your hands up on a straight-in slide.

A pop-up slide is usually the best slide when going into second on a steal because you can get up quickly and head toward third if the ball goes into the outfield.

Usually when you're stealing second base, you should use the pop-up slide, which is the one where as soon as you hit the bag with your right foot, you're coming up immediately. The advantage to the pop-up slide is that if the ball gets away from the man covering second, you are more likely to advance to third base. If you dive and the ball goes into the outfield, you're less likely to advance because you can't recover and get up as quickly. The pop-up slide was my favorite one as a player, because it got me right back on my feet again.

Many players today go headfirst into the base. I don't encourage that, mainly due to the possibility of injury. However, some players aren't as adept at sliding, so they dive headfirst into second base or third base. Ideally you want to use the straight-in slide, the pop-up slide or the hook slide if you can do it.

One thing you want to avoid at almost any cost is going headfirst into home plate. A lot of things can go wrong when your fingers or shoulders collide with the catcher's shin guards. Because of that, the hook slide is a good option at home plate. I NEVER recommend sliding headfirst into home plate.

We don't see the hook slide very much anymore, but it used to be very popular. One of my former teammates, Amos Otis, used to be very adept at it. In fact, he was probably the best hook slider I have ever seen. On the hook slide (Figure 4-9), you're actually sliding away from the bag with the intent to hook the bag with the top of your left foot. The only thing that ends up on the bag is the top of your left foot. The toe of that foot is on the corner of the bag. You have to be pretty good to use the hook slide effectively, but with practice you can do it.

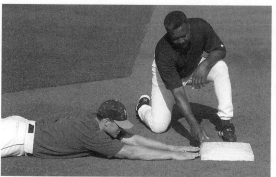 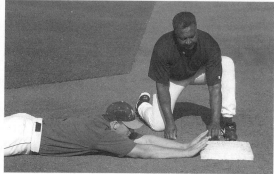

I'm not a fan of diving headfirst because several bad things can happen. Oftentimes, players jam their fingers into the bag (above left). If you must dive, you at least want to keep your fingers up as you go into the base (above right).

Figure 4-9

Signals to the hitter and runner

All base runners should know their responsibilities when they reach base. The best thing for a first-base coach to do when a runner initially gets on first is to make sure he is OK with the signs, and remind him of the number of outs. The first-base coach should also see where the outfielders are playing to let the runner know if he can possibly advance to third on a base hit. If there is a chance of the runner trying to steal second, the coach should let him know if the pitcher has any tendencies when throwing to first or the plate, and how quick the pitcher is to the plate.

The biggest problem runners at first seem to have is that they want to converse with the first baseman instead of watching the coach at third base, then they expect the first-base coach to let them know if they need to look for something. Therefore, the player's concentration at first base is not as good as it could and should be. It's unfortunate that more players put the pressure on the coach at first base to let them know what they should be doing, when they should be paying attention to the third-base coach themselves to know if any plays are on. The best advice I can give you is to know your team's signals and pay attention to your third-base coach giving the signs.

Conclusion

SPEED KILLS

Aggressive base running and team speed help make a team exciting and tough to beat. The old saying of "speed kills" applies to base running. You can force a lot of things with speed and good base running. Speed puts your team in an aggressive mode and forces the other team to have to look for advantages over you. Basically, speed and aggressive base running put a lot of pressure on the defense to be perfect and force them to do something they don't like to do—rush. As a batter-runner it's easier to speed yourself up than it is to slow yourself down. As a defensive player, it's easier to slow yourself down than it is to speed yourself up.

Teams that use their speed effectively on the base paths tend to speed up everyone else on the field and unsettle the defense. The infielders play closer than they normally would. For example, if a speedy player who can also bunt is at the plate, the third and first basemen come in on the corners and the middle infielders are at double-play depth instead of playing back. The infielders are automatically out of normal position

Willie Wilson

looking for a possible bunt. Willie Wilson of the Royals was so effective at getting infield hits, that then-Boston Red Sox manager Don Zimmer played his second baseman next to the pitcher's mound when Willie was at the plate.

Speed also instills a sense of urgency in a defense so that they must handle the ball cleanly and get rid of it, and their throws have to be on the mark. Speed makes pitchers divide their attention between the hitter and the base runner, which gives the hitter an advantage. The outfielders feel they have to make strong throws back to the infield on every ball to keep runners from taking extra bases. The catcher, with fast runners on base, calls for the pitcher to throw more fastballs than normal, because he wants an opportunity to throw the runner out.

Earlier in the book, in the chapter on defense, I talked about the importance of a defensive player anticipating what he would do if the ball were hit to him. Aggressive base running and speed help emphasize that point and show the importance of thinking ahead. Speed is important because it forces precision on defense. Any bobbled ball by the defensive player messes up the play.

With the speed of our Royals teams of the '70s and '80s, we used aggressive base running to our advantage. Whenever we hit a ball to the outfield and the centerfielder was going from left to right, we kept running. Teams with a good combination of offense, base runners and defense to go along with strong pitching are tough to beat. Those teams are exciting to watch.

Speed upsets the whole balance of defense. It creates an overall aggressive attitude from the whole team, not just from the fast players, and it creates a sense of fear in the defense because they know they have to be perfect. Next to pitching, speed and aggressive base running are the best weapons a team can have.

WHITE'S WORDS OF WISDOM

- Always know the rules of thumb that apply to base running.
- Know that if the ball is hit head high or lower you should freeze to make sure it gets through the infield to avoid being doubled up on a caught line drive.
- To avoid injury, never go headfirst into any base whenever possible.
- On a tag-up situation, always position yourself from one foot to the other so you can see around the infielder and have a good view of the outfielder making the catch.
- Always anticipate running from first to third on singles to the outfield.
- Always round first base on a base hit to make the outfielder stop you by securing the ball and getting it back to the infield.
- On balls to the hole at deep shortstop, know when you're going into second base to break up a double play and when you're going in to be safe. The approaches and slides are different.
- Always pay attention to the defense around you.

Chapter 5

"Let's Play Catch"

As I was scouting the "competition" before compiling *Good As Gold*, I discovered that there are very few non-pitching instructional books that include a large amount of information about throwing. The late Ken Dugan, a former college baseball coach in Tennessee, wrote a book that devoted an entire chapter to throwing. That was a rare exception. My co-author, Matt Fulks, became good friends with Dugan when the two worked together at Lipscomb University. Matt has told me that when Dugan was writing his book he said, "I can't believe there are all these instructional baseball books out there that don't talk a lot about throwing. How can you have an instructional book on baseball without talking about throwing?" Coach, I couldn't agree more. Without question, learning how to throw the baseball properly—the art of throwing—is a vital aspect in developing your baseball skills.

If you can throw hard and with accuracy, you can last a long time in this game. Both of those factors are key ingredients. If you're an outfielder with a strong arm but you can't hit the cut-off man, you're not as effective for your team, because the opposition will keep taking bases on you. If you're a pitcher who throws in the mid-90s, but you don't have any control, then you won't last in this game. A lot of players can throw 94 mph but they aren't in the major leagues because they can't control their fastballs through the strike zone.

As a non-professional, you should concentrate more on your accuracy and control instead of on how hard you can throw. Get your target and concentrate on throwing to it. Many times at the amateur level, players aren't wild throwers necessarily, but they just haven't learned good throwing mechanics from an outfielder-infielder standpoint or from a pitching standpoint.

Grappling gripping

The first thing you need to grasp (no pun intended) when learning how to throw a baseball properly is the way to hold it and grip it. When holding a baseball, you don't want to put a death grip on it. You need to have freedom to move your wrist and freedom to feel the ball come out of your hand and off your two fingertips when you throw it. However, children's hands might not be big enough yet to effectively hold the ball with only two fingers, so they should either use three fingers or grip it more in their palm. How tightly you grip a ball won't make a big difference until you're older and have a bigger hand and a stronger arm.

Ideally, at all levels you want to be able to hold the ball quickly and naturally using what is called a four-seam grip. For every position other than pitcher, the four-seam grip is the optimum grip for every throw that you make. The very first thing I encourage you to do is to take a baseball at home and just toss it up in the air with your throwing hand and experience different grips as you catch it. You can also drop a baseball on the floor or on your bed, and without looking at the ball, pick it up and get used to the proper grip. These are great training exercises, because in a game situation when you field the ball, you need to have an automatic feel for the grip.

You need to be able to grab the ball, feel the seams, and rotate it in your hands for the proper grip as you're going through your crow hop. Practice those two drills and get a feel for the ball, and the grip should become automatic for you.

GRIPS

The easiest way to describe the proper four-seam grip is to use a pitcher as an example. When a pitcher wants his fastball to sink, he holds it with a two-seam grip. That is, as the ball rotates in the air, only two seams are spinning backwards. That movement through the air, with a normal throw, causes the ball to sink down and away. If the pitcher wants the ball to sail up or across home plate, he still uses a two-seam grip, but he pulls down on the ball as he releases it. When he uses that two-seam grip, the ball usually doesn't have as much velocity even though it can have a lot of movement.

As infielders and outfielders, we don't want the ball to have any movement—other than straight—when we throw it. For that reason we always try to throw the ball across the seams with two fingers and the thumb, so as the ball travels through the air, all four seams are spinning backwards. Pitchers use

These are two ways that a pitcher would hold the ball with a two-seam grip.

The four-seam grip looks similar to the two-seam, except you hold the ball so that all four seams would spin back when you throw it.

a four-seam grip when they just want to throw a straight fastball to the outside or inside part of the plate. As fielders, when we use a four-seam grip, we get more carry on the ball, it stays straight, and it goes faster.

At a young age when you can't grip the ball with two fingers, you still want to use a four-seam grip, even though your throws will probably have a "hump"—they won't necessarily be straight, bullet throws. You may also need to grip the ball with three fingers. Again, these methods are fine until your hands get bigger and you develop more arm strength.

Younger players with smaller hands might need to grip the ball with three fingers.

The ball should be held comfortably in your hand.

Throwing mechanics

It's great and extremely valuable for kids to get out and simply play catch every day. One of the best ways to learn hand-eye coordination is by playing catch. I strongly encourage dads to go out with their sons—or big brothers to take their little brothers—and play catch every day, if possible. Baseball is a game that you have to practice a lot to become good at, because it's tough to master.

When you're playing catch with someone, you should always try to hit him or her in the chest area with your throws. Imagine an area on that person that goes from shoulder to shoulder, and chin to waist. To make playing catch more enjoyable, play a game involving a point system with your partner. For instance, every throw at the waist is worth one point; at the chest is worth two points; and at the head is worth three points. This is a way to help you concentrate—and have fun—while you're playing catch, instead of just standing there throwing the ball. We play that type of game at the major-league level during spring training to help the players with concentration and throwing fundamentals.

If you can't hit your partner in the chest as a young player, don't get too discouraged. Until your arm develops and gets stronger, it's tough to throw a ball that doesn't have that hump to it. On the flip side of that, if you're an older man—dad, older brother, uncle, coach, etc.—playing catch with these young players, you should throw the ball to them with some loft to it. Doing that gives the younger player a chance to see the ball as long as he can and react with a proper glove position. For instance, if the ball is at head level, the youngster probably already knows that he needs to hold the glove straight up. But if the ball is chest high, he might turn his glove with the palm up and try to catch it that way, in which case the ball will likely bounce off the heel of his glove and hit him in the lip. Experience and coaching teach him otherwise.

THE "ART" OF THROWING

Throwing is a two-step process—literally. The first step is a lead step toward your target, with your shoulder pointing in that direction (Figures 5-6 and 5-7). After you release the ball, the second step is to follow through with your back leg (Figure 5-8). Be sure to keep your eyes on the target.

As with gripping techniques, a pitcher is one of the best models to use for proper throwing mechanics. In order for a pitcher to throw a good strike, he has to be in line with the target, he has to get his shoulder turned in, he has to get his front leg up, he has to stride directly toward the target, and then he has

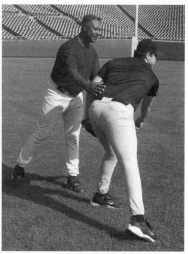

Figure 5-6   **Figure 5-7**   **Figure 5-8**

to follow through. Doing those things helps keep him in line to throw the ball where he wants it. For almost any good throw, balance is the key. When you're making a throw as a fielder, follow the pitcher's example, use a good range of motion, come over the top with your throw, and follow through, using your legs through the process.

The angle at which you have your arm when throwing depends on how far you have to throw and where you are on the field. If you have to make a long throw, e.g., as a shortstop, third baseman or an outfielder, you bring the ball high with at least a three-quarters arm angle (Figure 5-9). Throwing overhand helps you generate more power and velocity on your throws, it helps keep the ball straight, and it helps the ball ride (or carry) better. The lower you drop the angle of your arm, the more the ball will sink and veer away from the target (Figures 5-10 and 5-11).

Figure 5-9   **Figure 5-10**   **Figure 5-11**

FOLLOW THROUGH, FOLLOW THROUGH, FOLLOW THROUGH

We'll often see an infielder or an outfielder who makes a throw, and then re-coils his arm instead of following through. When you watch a pitcher throw, as he is making his delivery to the plate, his back leg follows through, which helps his pitch. Many infielders and outfielders will make a throw then leave their back leg behind instead of allowing their bodies to follow through. A major-league player with excellent follow through is outfielder Carlos Beltran. Whenever he has to make a long throw to third base or home plate he almost flips over and lands on his face after releasing the ball. This means that he's really following through on his throws. (If he lands spread-eagle on his chest, that's even better.)

Carlos Beltran

An infielder's follow through is different than an outfielder's. Besides the possibility of a second baseman throwing to first and being able to get away without following through— even though I don't recommend that—there are only a few instances when following through might not be possible. Those two instances revolve around the double play.

The first is on an exchange between the middle infielders. We don't really expect the shortstop or second baseman to follow through when making the throw to the player covering the second base bag. Then, on the throw from that player to first base, we don't expect a perfect follow through, especially if the runner from first is bearing down on him. For most all other times that you make a throw—regardless of your position—you need to follow through.

GLOVE POSITIONS

Besides throwing the ball, one detail you should work on whenever you're playing catch is the proper angle of your glove depending on where the ball is thrown to you. Even though it may seem simple enough for experienced players—and it is with practice—the proper way to catch a ball is a skill you need to master.

(Left) This is the proper glove angle if the ball is to you, above your waist. (Right) This is NOT the way to catch a ball above your waist.

If the ball is waist high or above, within a few inches of your body, you want to catch it with your glove as vertical as possible—depending on the ball's height. (It is OK to bend your knees slightly if the ball is a little below your waist.)

As the ball gets away from your body and you have to reach out farther, the angle of your glove will drop from vertical to horizontal (Figures 5-13, 5-13B and 5-13C).

Figure 5-13   Figure 5-13B   Figure 5-13C

Figure 5-14   Figure 5-14B   Figure 5-14C

If the ball is lower than your waist, you should turn the glove over, palm up, to make the catch (Figure 5-14). Your glove should remain palm up if the ball is below your waist and away from your body on your glove side (Figure 5-14B). But, you'll want to turn over your glove if the ball is low, away from your body and to your throwing side (Figure 5-14C). Always practice bending from the knees.

There may be exceptions to these rules, but knowing the most-used glove angles is an important skill to learn.

BREAKING IN THE GLOVE YOU'LL LOVE

Here are some practical steps that I used to pick my baseball gloves and ways you can get yours ready for action:

1. Find the leather you like and make sure that the laces are tight.

2. The glove shouldn't be too loose or too tight on your hand.

3. Most gloves already have some natural oil in them, but you want to condition the leather with glove oil. If you can't find glove oil, find a substance that includes lanolin, such as baby oil, shaving cream or hand lotion. I don't recommend dipping your glove in water, because the water can cause it to rot.

4. Play a lot of catch and then retighten the laces.

5. Always store your glove with a ball in it to help keep its form. Some players place a couple balls in their glove and then tie a belt or some string around it.

6. If the leather is hard, some players use a wooden mallet to beat the leather until it's supple enough. Treating your leather with respect (and common sense) should help give it a long life.

Throwing drills

DEVELOPING ARM STRENGTH

Playing catch and incorporating long throwing are the best ways to strengthen your throwing arm. From high school through the major leagues, pitchers throw in a game at a distance of 60 feet, six inches. Because of that, on their days off, major-league pitchers go to the outfield and play long catch to stretch out their arms. Outfielders have to throw a lot, especially at long distances, to keep their arms strong. Infielders should actually take a few steps back and throw from the outfield to strengthen their arms, even if they don't think it's necessary. Believe me, in a game situation when you have to make relay throws on a cut-off, you need good arm strength. When I was playing, there would be days that I would take infield practice from the outfield so I could work on making longer throws.

Before each game, non-pitchers should throw for at least 10 minutes. During that 10 minutes of work for outfielders, it is a good idea to work out to about 120 to 130 feet, and then work back in distance, to end with what is considered a "quick exchange," which is just like the move for middle infielders turning a double play.

On the quick exchange, stand less than 10 feet from the person you're playing catch with. All you have to do is take a step forward, catch the ball, and throw it right back to your partner. You want to toss the ball as fast as you can with touch and accuracy. This drill creates better hand-eye coordination and hand quickness. Working on that is especially beneficial to an outfielder when there's a situation where he has to get rid of the ball quickly, such as when a runner is tagging up.

Conclusion

GET THE LEAD OUT

I would be remissed if I finished this chapter without talking about getting your throwing arm ready after the off season. You want to come back slowly when you're starting to throw for the first time before a season. One of the best ways to make sure you don't overdo it at first is to time yourself throwing. For instance, during the first week or two, throw for only 10 minutes a day. Throw easy at first. In those first few days, your objective is to loosen your arm and its surrounding muscles. Also, during those first few days you don't want to throw the ball on the line. You should have some arc to your throws because you're simply trying to stretch out.

After the first day, you'll probably be a little bit stiff. That's normal. During the first few days, your arm will feel heavy when you're throwing. Then, for the next two or three days you'll start to feel your arm getting lighter and lighter. Before long you'll go through a dead-arm period, where your arm feels good but the ball's not really zinging at all. Finally, when your arm's in shape, everything feels good and the ball will "jump" for you. This stretching process takes about a week before you really want to throw the ball hard.

Players today have an advantage that I didn't have before reaching the major leagues. When my generation was growing up, we couldn't start throwing the ball until the weather was warmer, which, in the Midwest, can sometimes mean late March. Of course, players in places like Florida and Arizona could play nearly year-round. Today, players across the country can throw year-round with the help of indoor practice facilities that are open to the public. If you have access to one of these facilities, I encourage you to take advantage of it. Your arm will thank you for it.

WHITE'S WORDS OF WISDOM

- Always try to use a four-seam grip.
- Always step toward your target.
- Always follow through on your throws.
- As an outfielder on a tag-up situation, make sure you get behind the ball, and then bring the ball over the top and throw it low, always trying to hit your cut-off man.
- As an infielder, never throw a ball when you don't have a proper grip. It's better to just miss a runner and keep him at that base than to throw the ball with a bad grip and give him an extra base on a bad throw.

Chapter 6

Championship Conditioning

Staying in shape, conditioning your body with exercise and good nutrition in most cases will determine how long you'll play a sport. You may not reach the level you would like, but physically you would still be able to play. I was able to not only play on Astroturf for 18 years, but also play in more than 2,000 major-league games because I worked out year-round, every other day. Staying in shape is vital to longevity and good health.

MY BEST ADVICE

"A large part of the reason I was able to play until I was 45 was that I did a lot of arm exercises that weren't strenuous. I used a three-pound ball and did exercises that were recommended."
— *Gaylord Perry, pitcher, who was inducted into the Baseball Hall of Fame in 1991, with more than 300 wins and 3,500 strikeouts*

I didn't focus on complete weight training until 1983—10 years into my big-league career—when the Royals moved me to the third and fourth spots in the hitting order. Until that time, I concentrated on working my shoulders and forearms to help me in throwing and hitting. I did a lot of sit-ups to keep my back strong for our stadium's artificial turf, plus a lot of leg lifts and squats to keep my legs and knees strong for the turf. For today's players, however, there are many types of exercise equipment available to help you stay in tip-top shape for longer periods of time so you don't fatigue as much. In turn, if you don't fatigue as much, you're less prone to "nagging" injuries.

THESE TIMES, THEY ARE A'CHANGING

Teams' attitudes have changed over the years regarding conditioning. Most teams today in the major leagues have a full-time strength and conditioning coach and an assistant. Some organizations even have strength and conditioning coaches for their minor-league teams. Tim Maxey runs the strength and conditioning program for the Cleveland Indians. I think he has one of the best programs in the league. Before joining the Indians, Tim worked in a similar capacity with the Royals. Injuries in terms of muscle pulls, back spasms and similar nagging problems were greatly decreased when Tim started working with the Royals.

With a good program like Tim's, players maintain their strength throughout the season, including the toughest stretch—August through September.

Tim puts the players on a thorough daily program starting in spring training that lasts through the year. It's not uncommon for players to be in the weight room after a ballgame. The players who are serious about improving their game follow Tim's program religiously.

In the off season, he gives all of the players a training manual that they use from October until spring training. When spring training rolls around, you can always tell who has stuck with Tim's program during the off season, and who hasn't. The benefit of Tim's year-round schedule is obvious because our players stayed healthy during the long season.

Since things have changed—and continue to change—considerably in baseball conditioning since I played, Tim will help me guide you through the rest of this chapter. He will be providing quotes, suggested workout programs and "Maxey's Maxims," which are important ideas for you to keep in mind for your baseball conditioning and nutrition programs.

BEFORE YOU GET STARTED

As Tim advises young players: Safety is the most important thing for any strength and conditioning program. Safety includes consulting your physician before starting a program, knowing at what age to start lifting with any type of external resistance, using proper form, and having an experienced spotter present when you work out with weights. Generally, junior high is thought to be a good age to start training with external resistance, although you can initiate training as early as 10 or 11 years old with supervision and no weights added to the bar.

Regardless of when you start lifting weights, you should definitely focus on proper lifting technique before you add any type of resistance. Don't worry about what the guy next to you is lifting. Increase weight according to your body, your needs and your experience. If you're a beginner, you probably won't be able to lift as much as the guy who has been strength training for several years. The benefits of your workout should far outweigh the cost of possibly getting injured.

You also need to set goals before starting a program. The goals of your strength and conditioning program should be to improve athletic performance on the field, aggressively prevent injuries, and to reach your individual full potential.

MAXEY'S MAXIMS

Cost-to-Benefit Ratio
For every exercise or drill that you incorporate into your program, the benefit of that exercise or drill must far outweigh the potential for injury.

SIZE DOESN'T MATTER

You don't have to be the Incredible Hulk to be a good baseball player. Actually, you don't want to be that big. You want to strengthen your muscles, but you don't have to develop a ton of size in the process. You should think in terms of baseball performance instead of bodybuilding. Baseball muscles are supposed to be straight and strong.

We're not bodybuilders or power lifters; we're baseball players. You want to be as athletic as possible for your body. Our guys train heavy year-round, which includes in season, but it's according to the individual and his experience. We wouldn't expect a 25-year-old with one year of training experience to lift the same as a 25-year-old with 10 years of experience in training. That's a big mistake that coaches make at every level. Your baseball workout should emphasize strength over size. Tim uses the example that if a player weighs 175 pounds, that guy should strive to be the strongest 175-pound person possible. If a guy weighs 225 pounds, he should try to be the strongest 225-pound player possible.

Bodybuilding-type programs can hurt your flexibility, which is important in defense and hitting. Strength training with free weights using a full range of motion has the potential to improve your flexibility. At the same time, muscular strength can help curb fatigue and fight some injuries.

SHOULDERING THE LOAD

I worked on maintaining shoulder strength throughout my career, year-round. Very few injuries in baseball can hurt your performance more than an injury to your shoulder, especially your throwing shoulder. Maxey uses what he calls the "Elite Eight Shoulder Program." These are exercises that should be performed year-round, with the idea that you do them daily during the off season, and four or five days a week during your baseball season. Please remember that this program is not to build size; it is to develop the strength of your various shoulder muscles.

—Standing Flexion: Arm at side, thumb forward, raise your arm forward and continue straight overhead. Thumb should be pointing behind you at the end of the movement. Slowly return to the starting position.

Everyone should begin with two to three pounds and do 10 reps of all eight exercises. Regardless of your age, your maximum weight should be five pounds with one set of 10 reps.

—Standing Supraspinatus: Thumb at corner of front pocket. With thumb down, raise arm to just below shoulder height. The arm should stay at an angle that will return the thumb to the same point.

—Scaption with External Rotation: Begin in same position as previous, except turn thumb up so heel of hand is at the corner of the pocket. Slowly raise weight up to the side, continuing overhead. Then slowly return to the starting point.

—External Rotation/Prone Abduction: Lie on table or lean over at waist until chest is parallel with floor. Throwing arm hangs straight down from shoulder. Turn thumb up and raise arm out to side to shoulder height. Slowly return.

—Prone Scaption: Lie on table or lean over at waist until chest is parallel with floor. Arm hangs straight down from shoulder. Slowly, bring weight up to the level of the tabletop, and then return to starting point.

—Prone Extension: Lie face down on table. Throwing arm hanging straight down from shoulder, set scapula (shoulder blade), turn palm to floor and bring arm up next to your side. Slowly return.

—Internal Rotation (USE ONLY ONE TECHNIQUE PER SESSION):
Internal Rotation Tubing: Place towel roll or glove between arm and body. Bend elbow to 90 degrees with upper arm slightly away from chest. May use towel roll between arm and chest. Pull tubing in across body, allow arm to return to starting position slowly.

Internal Rotation Dumbbell: Lay on side with upper arm on table and elbow bent to 90 degrees. Rotate at shoulder and bring weight up toward abdomen. Slowly return to starting position.

—External Rotation (USE ONLY ONE TECHNIQUE PER SESSION):
External Rotation Tubing: Place towel roll or glove between arm and body. Bend elbow to 90 degrees with upper arm slightly away from chest and hand in front of stomach. Pull tubing out toward the side, allow arm to return to the starting position slowly.

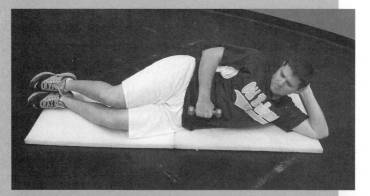

External Rotation Dumbbell: Lay on side with upper arm at side, elbow bent to 90 degrees and hand in front of stomach. "Set" scapula (shoulder blade) and rotate at shoulder lifting weight toward ceiling. Slowly return to starting position.

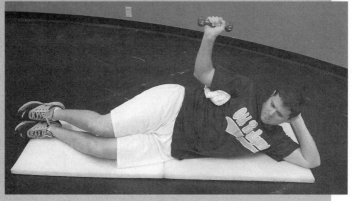

The exercises

The next several pages, in Tim's words, explain and illustrate the suggested exercises for this chapter. You might use this section as a reference guide once we outline sample in-season and off-season strength and conditioning programs later in the chapter.

STRENGTH TRAINING FROM TIM MAXEY

MAXEY'S MAXIMS

Core strength is essential for a baseball player. The core of your body includes hips, legs and trunk. Everyone thinks that you should develop your arms—biceps and triceps—before worrying about core strength. It's actually the opposite. As a baseball player, you need to develop your core strength before worrying about your "beach" muscles.

TM: An athlete's body functions as a whole. Your strength and conditioning program should be based on exercises and drills involving multiple-joint actions to improve athletic performance. As an athlete it doesn't make a lot of sense to focus on one muscle group, such as biceps, when that muscle group will rarely be working alone during competition.

Use major exercises to work the body as a whole, improving total body functions and coordination. The three most important lifts (the major exercises) for a baseball player are: 1.) The squat—plus variations; 2.) The lunge—plus variations; and 3.) Back exercises.

Squats and lunges are important because they are ground-based exercises using free weights, meaning you are applying force with the feet against the ground. The more force you can apply against the ground, the more effective you will become in sport skills such as running, fielding and throwing. Machines are not as good, because when you use them, you're not applying that force to the ground during the exercise. Training your back muscles is important because they are the decelerators, or "brakes," of your body, especially when it comes to throwing. We usually perform two back exercises for every one chest exercise.

Minor exercises, such as bicep curls and tricep extensions, work stabilizer muscles (the muscles involved indirectly in action), which help keep the foundation stable and prevent injuries. We usually perform one minor exercise per strength workout.

Using free weights on the following exercises will help teach balance and awareness. This helps make the transfer of strength and power easier to merge with the development of sport skills when you are on the field.

—**SQUAT:** The squat requires proper technique to receive the full benefits of the exercise and to prevent injury. If you feel that your form is not correct, do another exercise such as the hip sled. This exercise will develop the quadriceps, gluteus maximus and hamstrings.

Resting the bar behind your neck with the shoulder blades drawn together and your back flat (not arched), take a deep breath and hold it. Slowly squat down to a position where the middle of the thigh is parallel or near parallel to the ground. Return to the starting position by extending the legs. Your head, chest and back should remain on the same plane going up as they were coming down. Exhale your breath as you near the completion of the lift. Complete the squat by fully extending the legs to the starting position. *Caution:* Resting the bar on the trapezius muscle is very important. If the bar is not rested properly, too much weight could cause stress to the shoulder joint.

—**LUNGE:** The lunge is another exercise that will develop the muscles of the thighs and hips.

Start with the bar on your back, similar to the starting position for the squat. (You may also perform this exercise with dumbbells, holding them at your side.) Your feet should be less than shoulder width apart. Begin the exercise by stepping forward with one foot, while the rear foot stays planted. You should step far enough that the lower part of your front leg is perpendicular to the ground. Lower your hips until the back knee is approximately two inches from the ground. The lower leg remains perpendicular to the ground throughout the movement. Push back with the forward foot and return it to the starting position without dragging it on the ground. Step forward with the opposite foot and repeat.

—**LEG PRESS:** The leg press works the same muscles as the squat—quadriceps, hamstrings and gluteus maximus. Since this is a major exercise, it could be used in place of the squat or lunge if you do not have good technique on those exercises or do not feel comfortable doing them.

Start on your back with head and shoulders comfortably on the hip sled board. Place your feet at the desired width apart on the footrest. Make sure the

locking mechanism is engaged. Adjust the board to the appropriate level according to your height. To perform the exercise, move the carriage up the 45-degree angle track by extending the legs. Lower the carriage slowly and repeat.

—**LAT PULLDOWNS:** Lat pulldowns will develop the latissimus dorsi muscle (the area that extends across the outer part of your upper and middle back).

Use a sitting or kneeling position when performing the machine lat pulldown. Your palms should be facing out with a wide grip. Allow the weight to pull upward on the shoulders and lats while the arms are straight. Pull with your elbows pointing downward and slightly back. (You may also perform this exercise with a reverse grip, with your hands approximately 12 inches apart and facing in. For this position, pull the bar downward in front of the face and to the top of the chest.) This exercise should be done slowly and smoothly. *Caution:* Do not use momentum and swing the weight. That type of movement could injure the back or shoulder area.

—**SEATED (LOW) ROWS:** This exercise will develop the muscles of the middle and upper back. A low pulley is required for this exercise, although it could also be performed on hammer strength machines.

Use a seated position facing the machine. Position the torso at a 90-degree angle to the floor, slightly bend the knees, and allow the weight to extend your elbows. With your back straight, pull the bar or handle toward your chest and upper abdomen, keeping your elbows close to your body. Allow the bar or handle to move slowly and under control away from your body. Exhale on the backward movement. *Caution:* Do not use momentum and swing the weight. That type of movement could injure the back or shoulder area.

—**DUMBBELL ROWS:** The dumbbell row is another exercise that works your latissimus dorsi muscle. The nice thing is that it requires only a flat bench and dumbbells.

Kneel on the bench with your inside leg and lean forward, placing your inside hand on the bench in front of your outside leg. The outside leg should be planted firmly, with the knee bent slightly. Your back should be flat with your head facing up. The dumbbell should be held forward slightly, stretching the lat muscle. Slowly draw the dumbbell up and back, keeping your elbow close to the body, with your shoulders even and parallel to the ground. Lower the dumbbell slowly and under control to the stretched starting position. *Caution:* Do not use momentum and swing the weight. That type of movement could injure the back or shoulder area.

—DUMBBELL BENCH PRESS: This exercise will develop the pectoral muscle with minor emphasis on the deltoids and triceps. The exercise can be performed on an adjustable bench or a flat bench.

Position your feet flat on the floor, while lying face up on the bench. Your head, shoulders and buttocks should be flat on the bench throughout the entire movement. From an inclined position, the dumbbells are grasped and held above the chin at arm's length, with palms facing forward, six to eight inches apart. (To reduce strain on the shoulders, you can also face palms toward your body.) Inhale as the dumbbells are lowered to the shoulder, the elbows extended to the side. Exhale as the weight is pressed slightly back and upward at the same time. *Caution:* Remember to avoid bouncing the weight off your chest, raising your hips off the bench, or lowering the dumbbells too far down on the chest.

—CLOSE GRIP BENCH PRESS: This exercise will develop the chest and tricep muscles, both of which assist the baseball player in acceleration of the arm during hitting and throwing. The dumbbell bench press could serve as an alternate exercise if previous shoulder injuries restrict the use of the close grip bench press.

Obtain a grip on the bar where your index fingers are approximately 12 inches apart. (This means that the first two fingers of each hand are on the smooth part of an Olympic bar.) Lower the bar until it touches your chest, keeping your elbows at the sides. Return the bar to the starting position by pushing it off the chest to a fully locked position. *Caution:* A rolled towel can be placed on the chest to restrict the range of motion.

—**DUMBBELL SHOULDER ROUTINE:** The dumbbell shoulder routine is a combination of three exercises. Each exercise works a different head of the deltoid muscle—anterior, lateral and posterior. Start by doing front raises for 10 repetitions, then do lateral raises for 10 repetitions, and end with bent-over raises for 10 repetitions. These exercises are to be performed consecutively without a break between each exercise. Five- to 15-pound dumbbells will be used generally. Younger players and other less experienced lifters should use lighter weight.

FRONT RAISES

FRONT RAISES: Begin with a dumbbell in each hand, with your arms hanging in front of your body. Your palms should be facing in and the dumbbells should be resting on the front of the thigh. Raise the dumbbells to shoulder level, keeping your palms facing down and your hands in front of your body. There should be a slight bend in the arms that remains constant throughout the exercise. Lower the dumbbells and repeat.

LATERAL RAISES: Begin with a dumbbell in each hand, with your palms facing in and the dumbbells resting on the outside of your thighs. Raise the dumbbells to shoulder level, keeping the palms facing down. Your hands should be raised directly to the side, staying in the midline of the body. Lower the dumbbells and repeat.

LATERAL RAISES

BENT-OVER RAISES

BENT-OVER RAISES: Bend forward at the waist until your upper body is parallel to the floor. There should be a slight bend in the knees. Your arms should be hanging straight down with your palms facing each other. From this position, raise the dumbbells upward to the side and forward slightly, until your arms are parallel to the ground. Lower the dumbbells to the starting position and repeat. Each repetition should be performed smoothly and slowly on the up and down movements.

MAXEY'S MAXIMS

You make more progress over longer periods of time if you do not work at maximum loads during each workout. Using a "Hard-Medium" system eliminates over-training and mental burnout, because the first two workout days of the week are the heavy workouts, while the other days are lighter workouts.

ABDOMINALS

Strengthening your abdominals should be a major goal year-round. They support and protect your internal organs, as well as provide support for the postural muscles of your lower back. As a baseball player, you generate force with your legs and apply it through your arms. However, this energy is transferred through your midsection. Since you are only as strong as your weakest link, poorly developed abdominals can actually lead to arm problems down the road.

ABDOMINAL GROUP—1

Exercise:	*To Perform:*
Bent Knee Crunch	Hands behind head
Straight Leg Crossover	Legs 6-10 inches off ground
Cross-Leg Crunch	Knees bent, feet crossed
Bicycle Pedaling	Legs 6-10 inches off ground

ABDOMINAL GROUP—2

Exercise:	*To Perform:*
Bent Knee Reach-Through	
Straight Leg Lift	Alternate legs up and down
Alternate Elbow-Knee	Elbow to opposite knee
Bent Knee Lifts	Knees to chest, feet to ground

AGILITY

One of the most important physical aspects of baseball that Tim Maxey stresses is agility. An agile player is able to move swiftly and change directions quickly and fluidly. Examples would be a runner rounding the bases, an infielder turning a double play, or an outfielder cutting off a ball in the alley and holding the hitter to a single. In order to improve the power to change directions quickly, the legs should not be fatigued. If your legs are tired, the contraction will be too slow to improve the power necessary for the rapid movements. This is why agility work should be done at the same time as your speed work. In fact, doing agility work first will serve as a warm up for the speed drills. Give yourself enough rest between each run to move as fast and sharp as possible on the next drill.

—**60-YARD SHUTTLE:** For this drill you need a course with four lines five yards apart (15 yards total with one line as your starting point). From the starting line, sprint to the first line (five yards), touch it with your hand and backpedal to the start line. Sprint to the second line (10 yards), touch it with your hand and backpedal to the start line. Then, sprint to the third line (15 yards), touch it with your hand and backpedal until you cross the start line.

—**PRO AGILITY DRILL:** For this drill, use the same 15-yard course, but mark it with one line in the middle. Straddle the middle line, facing one of the other lines. Sprint to that line and touch it with your hand. Push off forcefully and sprint across to the far line and touch it with your opposite foot. Sprint back, finishing at the middle line.

MAXEY'S MAXIMS

OVERLOAD vs. OVER-TRAINING
Allow sufficient rest. Don't be hard headed when the body needs less work.

SPEED

Baseball is a sport that requires quick bursts of speed—running out an infield grounder, chasing a ball in the gap, trying to beat the batter-runner to first base. Speed is important for EVERY baseball player. Speed itself cannot be taught, but the techniques to develop speed skills can be.

Like other skills, to develop speed skills you need to practice with proper technique and at game speed. To create speed, you need to apply the greatest possible force onto the ground in the shortest possible time. Improved hip and leg strength (squats and lunges) will enhance your ability to apply the big forces onto the ground, thereby moving your body more efficiently. Secondly, to develop speed you have to train hard and fast with full recovery between sprints (approximately one to two minutes).

SPEED WORK GUIDELINES

1. Never do leg strength training before full speed work. **2.** Full recovery between sprints is essential. **3.** Train hard and fast. **4.** Quality vs. Quantity!

—**CUT 60s:** Sprint out 30 yards (90 feet), then sprint back to the starting point. Your goal should be to finish each rep in between nine and 11 seconds. With that in mind, for a full recovery between reps (sprints) you should rest for approximately 27 to 33 seconds (three parts rest to one part work). We generally run these in the outfield corner.

—**FLYING 20s:** Mark off 40 yards with some type of designation at 20 yards. Start running at half speed, building speed with each stride for 20 yards. By the time you reach the 20-yard point, you should be running at full speed. Continue to sprint for the next 20 yards. Again, be sure to rest between runs.

LIMBER UP

An often overlooked aspect of a complete conditioning program is stretching and flexibility. Before a game or practice, players need to get warm and stretch everything! Calves, arms, shoulders, and even the neck—every part of the body should be stretched. After stretching, our guys go through a 10-minute warm-up program for throwing, and then they run to get the legs warm and ready to go. Since baseball is such a stop-and-go sport, you want to be as loose and limber as possible when you take the field.

One thing to remember before starting any type of athletic event is that you have to get your body properly loose for the event itself. Ballplayers need to come out before a game or practice and stretch their bodies to get ready for the day's activities. Your goal before you start your pregame throwing is to have your body warmed up and muscles stretched. As Tim puts it, you want to "get your engine revved up." So the first thing you want to do is raise your body's core temperature by going through some light jogging, jump rope, or some other similar activity that will start to loosen all of your muscles.

After you have completed your warm up, go directly into your stretches, spending only about 10 to 20 seconds per body part. A good way to make sure you stretch everything is to start at the top and work your way down. Once that is done you should be ready to start your pregame or prepractice throwing. Again, it's important to do the warm up before the stretching in order to get good blood flow and be more elastic.

SKILL WORK

FW: In order to become a better baseball player, you obviously need to practice. You need to work on sport-specific skills—fielding ground balls, catching fly balls, throwing, hitting, etc.—nearly every day. The more you practice your skills, and practice with proper technique, the quicker you will improve as a player. As you read through the workouts listed later in this chapter, you will see how skill work is built into various programs. In much the same way that weight workouts train your muscles to get stronger, skill work teaches your muscles the proper feeling of performing a certain action, such as fielding a ground ball.

Back when I played, most of the players didn't even pick up a baseball until January, the month before spring training. Today, more professional teams are placing their players on intense off-season programs that include skill work.

It's important to take a little time off at the end of a season to recuperate. Your body definitely needs the rest if you have an intense season. However, the more time you take off after you're rested, the more "rusty" you'll be in your baseball skills.

You might be wondering how in the world you're going to work on your skills in the fall and winter. Obviously the weather and your other school activities will determine how much time you can spend on your skill work before spring. As I mention throughout this book, and as you're probably aware, a lot of cities have indoor facilities where you can work on your hitting, and sometimes on your fielding, during the off season.

You can also be inventive in your training. When I was in the Baseball Academy, we had a tire nailed to a tree that we hit to develop forearm and back strength. Then we'd go to a handball court—although virtually any brick wall will work—with our gloves and a ball, and throw the ball off the wall and field it, working on stance and proper fielding technique. If possible, try to find some way to work on your technique to make sure that you don't lose all of your skills during the off season by not doing anything.

As you work on your baseball skills, operate at two different speeds—technique and game. "Technique speed" means that you're going through the motions and practicing at a speed that allows you to focus on proper technique and fundamentals. "Game speed" means that you're going as hard as you would if it were a tied ballgame in the last inning. Again, those are ways to make your muscles know how to react once you are in a game situation.

TIM'S FINAL THOUGHTS ON THE EXERCISES

TM: Those are the main exercises and drills you will use to get in (and stay in) the best possible baseball shape. Even though time will not always allow you to follow strict programs such as the ones that follow, for baseball you should strive to reach a good combination of work in strength training, abdominal work, conditioning, stretching, and skill work at least four days a week.

In-season training

FW: The attitude about in-season conditioning and weight training has changed quite a bit through the years. When I was playing, what we did in the weight room on our own time was our complete weight workout. We weren't on any type of team weight lifting "program." Most of us at that time did more cardiovascular exercises than weight work. In fact, we didn't have weights with the Royals until 1983. The complete conditioning phase of the game is more important now to help players stay healthy and competitive.

BUILDING UP TO AVOID BREAKING DOWN

TM: Most people do their "grunt" or "grind" workouts during the off season. That's when they change their bodies. Then when the season rolls around, they stop working out. What they have done is started the season at a high level physically, maybe the best shape they've ever been in, but they fatigue because they aren't training during the season.

Part of what makes a great athlete is durability. In terms of baseball, a coach obviously wants his best nine players on the field at all times. Over the course of a season, at any playing level, fatigue and the risk of injury can go way up. One way to fight that is with in-season strength training, which, along with a sound nutrition program, will prevent some of the injuries.

Some players start the season thinking that they want to simply maintain their strength, speed and conditioning through the season. I don't like the term "maintain" for in-season workouts. Why maintain? Why not get stronger? The biggest difference between your off-season and in-season workouts is that there is a reduction of the intensity (weight) and volume (sets and reps) during the baseball season. Strength gains can happen, but the results are slower compared to an off-season program. You should strive to stay strong or get stronger as the season progresses. Most of our players get stronger in season, which helps them toward the end of the year. However, remember that the time you have to dedicate toward in-season lifting and conditioning might be different than it is for a major-league player.

IMPORTANCE OF STRENGTH TRAINING

FW: As Tim mentioned, strength training is important throughout the season to help you avoid injuries. Many older coaches feel that working out with weights can cause a player to get too big to play baseball. And, yes, there is some truth to the old-school thought that players who do a lot of chest exercises can bulk up too much and end up hurting their performance. Most players who lift weights do not emphasize the chest area. You don't want your chest to get too big, because you have to throw across that part of your body. However, if you follow a strength program like Tim's, you should be able to notice the benefits during the baseball season.

The aggressive way to prevent injuries is strength training. Injuries occur when an athlete is placed in a position where the force acting upon him is more than he is able to resist. Strength training minimizes the chance that this can happen.

The most important factor in your development is that you rarely miss a workout. Be consistent. Consistency and commitment are the keys to gaining strength. During the season you obviously will spend more time on practice and competition and less on your strength and conditioning. However, use your time wisely, do quality work, and commit to a program.

MAXEY'S MAXIMS

A stronger athlete is less likely to be injured.

GENERAL GUIDELINES
FOR IN-SEASON WEIGHT TRAINING

1. You should work major muscle exercises. **2.** You should work each muscle group twice a week. **3.** You should do three or four sets of each exercise. **4.** You should never increase the intensity (weight) and volume (reps) at the same time. **5.** You should increase the weight progressively during the in-season program, but vary the sets and reps.

MAXEY'S MAXIMS

PUSH/PULL THEORY—The PUSH/PULL system is a simple way to set up a workout so that you never work the same muscle group two days in a row.

PUSH	PULL
Chest	Back
Legs	Shoulders
Triceps	Biceps

THE IN-SEASON WORKOUT

The following is a one-week sample of an in-season strength and conditioning program. Since you'll be doing this during the season, the strength portion of the workout is done two days a week, keeping in mind that you don't want to lift on consecutive days and you don't want to lift earlier in the day before a game.

You should perform three or four sets of each strength exercise focusing on major exercises first, then minor exercises. The following example is based on three sets. The number of reps for each exercise is listed to the right. The major exercises were explained earlier in the chapter. The specific exercises you do for biceps and triceps is up to you, although you'll continue to do only three sets of 10 reps as you progress through the workouts. Based on the previous guidelines and your experience, as you progress through the strength portion of this workout, you should try to increase the weight. Remember to always have a spotter and/or a workout partner with you for safety and to help you reach your maximum potential.

DAY ONE

Cut 60s	6-8	Squat or Leg Press	3x6
Leg Curls	3x10	Dumbbell Bench Press	3x8
Lat Pulldown	3x10	Dumbbell Row	3x8
Tricep Exercise	3x10	Bicep Exercise	3x10
Forearms			

Abdominal Group 1
Shoulder Routine
Elite Eight Routine

DAY TWO

Flying 20s	6-8	Lunges	3x6
Leg Curls	3x10	Dumbbell Incline	3x8
Lat Pulldown	3x10	Low Row	3x8
Bicep Exercise	3x10	Tricep Exercise	3x10

Forearms
Shoulder Routine
Abdominal Group 2
Elite Eight Routine

DAY THREE

Cardio Flush   (Bike or jog for 20 minutes. Can be performed outside, or on a machine stationary bike or treadmill inside.)

MAXEY'S MAXIMS

Practice makes perfect, but only if you practice perfect.

Off-season training

FW: When I was playing, I worked out A LOT during the off season. I took about two weeks off at the end of the season and then went back to work. Most of our work with teammates came right after New Year's Day. That is when we started to hit and throw. In the past players went to spring training to get in shape, but today's players have to be ready to go as soon as they get there. Today, training is a year-round commitment for professional players. Even for amateurs, with competition being so fierce for college baseball scholarships, players are working out harder and longer, trying to get in shape for spring try-outs.

Off season is the time to improve your overall baseball conditioning, especially if you don't participate in any other sports during the fall and winter. The goal of your off-season program should be to get in the best baseball shape possible for the next season.

In our philosophy today, a player has a responsibility to prepare himself during the off season. The off season and preseason are the most intense times of the year in terms of training. Although it is apparent some uniquely gifted players are able to be successful even when their approaches to training are obviously not optimal, it is clear that such players cannot achieve their full potential in baseball without improving their physical capacity to play the game.

The following sample program is designed to help improve your performance on the field, reduce the chance of injury, and reach your individual full potential. As we've mentioned in this chapter, the level of baseball you're playing will determine the amount of time you're able to spend getting ready for the next baseball season. If you're an amateur, your off season might include school activities, other sports such as football and basketball, your baseball coach's training program, and, of course, your homework and study time.

MY BEST ADVICE:

"Very early in my career, I noticed players getting hurt in spring training because they didn't do much conditioning in the off season. I made the parallel that players would get out of shape in the off season and then, while trying to get in baseball shape during spring training, they'd get injured. I made a promise to myself that I was going to approach my career where I never would be out of shape. I tried to get in better shape during the off season, and then go into spring training each year in better shape than I was the year before. It's not as traumatic to do explosive baseball moves when you're in shape. You're putting yourself at risk of injury when you try to do those things out of shape."
——*Cal Ripken Jr., baseball's "Iron Man," who played in 2,632 consecutive games*

OFF-SEASON CONDITIONING

TM: Baseball requires intense bursts of short speed. In order to improve speed conditioning, you should train in a similar manner—intense periods of conditioning with rest intervals built in. This type of training will allow you to recover between plays and pitches and therefore be able to give 100 percent on every play.

In order to prepare your energy system for this intense off-season work, you must first build a base of aerobic conditioning. The aerobic conditioning will make your energy system more efficient so that as you progress through the program's phases, your body will be able to recover. This conditioning program is progressive in nature. You should follow each phase as stated so that your body will be ready as the program's intensity builds. Although any of the running workouts can be performed on any surface, it would be best if you run on grass as much as possible.

PHASE 1: DISTANCE RUNNING

The first phase of the program builds your aerobic base. To accomplish this, you should run two to two and a half miles in less than 23 minutes. If you don't have a set course of this distance, use a car to make your own route—or have someone drive the course for you. This phase lasts only two weeks and could reduce your muscular strength and power if continued for a longer period of time.

PHASE 2: TIMED LAPS

Timed laps are run on a baseball field from home plate toward right field, around the warning track to the left field foul pole. (This is approximately 300 yards on a high school or older baseball field.) Each timed lap is just as it sounds—one lap in 1:15 to 1:25. The rest interval between each run is one minute and 15 seconds. Remember, don't expect to be able to handle the same workload as someone with experience. For instance, a freshman probably won't be able to handle the same amount as a senior. That's a huge mistake that coaches make. This phase also lasts two weeks.

PHASE 3: SPRINTS

The third phase of the conditioning program is the sprint section. This is where your work from the distance running, and timed laps helps prepare you for those intense bursts of speed that are associated with baseball. Throughout this phase you will be running 200- and 110-yard sprints. Again, based on the size of at least a high school field, the 200s are from one foul pole to centerfield and back. The 110s are from a foul pole to slightly past centerfield.

LAYING IT OUT

Four-day Split Routine with Running

MON	TUE	WED	THUR	FRI
Skill Work	Skill Work	Rest	Skill Work	Skill Work
Speed Work	Chest	(Stretch)	Chest	Triceps
Shoulders	Back	Speed Work	Triceps	Legs
Back	Biceps	Shoulders	Conditioning	
Conditioning		Legs		
		Biceps		

PUTTING IT ALL TOGETHER: THE WORKOUT

FW: The following is a sample of an eight-week, four-day routine that Tim Maxey uses for the Indians during the off season. Tim and his staff individualize a program for each player. This sample program's goal is to prepare you for the upcoming season. The number of sets and reps for each exercise is listed to the right. Most of the exercises are explained earlier in the chapter. The exercises you do for biceps and triceps is up to you. Always have a spotter and/or a workout partner with you for safety and to help you reach your maximum potential. This sample should be altered according to your experience, years of training, and the amount of time you have to prepare. Many factors come in to play for your schedule. Remember that the benefits of any exercise you do should far outweigh the cost of getting injured, the cost-to-benefit ratio.

EXERCISE DAY & NAME	WEEKS 1 & 2	WEEKS 3 & 4	WEEKS 5 & 6	WEEKS 7 & 8
MONDAY				
Pro Agility Drill/				
Cut 60s	6-8	6-8	6-8	6-8
Squat or Leg Press	3x10	4x5	4x8	4x5
Leg Curls	3x10	4x8	4x10	4x8
Lat Pulldowns	3x10	4x8	4x10	4x8
Low Rows	3x10	4x8	4x10	4x8
Shrugs	3x20	3x20	3x20	3x20
Bicep Exercise	3x10	3x10	3x10	3x10
Abdominal Group 1				
TUESDAY				
Bench or				
Dumbbell Press	3x10	4x5	4x8	4x5
Dumbbell Incline	3x10	4x5	4x8	4x5
Incline Flys	3x10	4x10	4x8	4x10
Tricep Exercise	3x10	3x10	3x10	3x10
Shoulder Routine	3x10	4x10	4x8	4x8
Forearms	3x10	4x10	4x10	4x10
Abdominal Group 2				
Conditioning	2-2.5 mi.	10/300	12/200	22/110
THURSDAY				
60 Yard Shuttle/				
Flying 20s	6-8	6-8	6-8	6-8
Lunges or Leg Press	3x10	4x5	4x8	4x5
Leg Curls	3x10	4x8	4x10	4x8
Lat Pulldowns	3x10	4x8	4x10	4x8
Dumbbell Rows	3x10	4x8	4x10	4x8
Shrugs	3x20	3x20	3x20	3x20
Bicep Exercise	3x10	3x10	3x10	3x10
Abdominal Group 1				

FRIDAY

Incline Press	3x10	4x5	4x8	4x5
Close-Grip Bench Press	3x10	4x5	4x8	4x5
Dumbbell Flat Flys	3x10	4x10	4x8	4x10
Tricep Exercise	3x10	3x10	3x10	3x10
Shoulder Routine	3x10	4x10	4x8	4x8
Forearms	3x10	4x10	4x10	4x10
Abdominal Group 2				
Conditioning	2-2.5 mi.	10/300	12/200	22/110

Nutrition

FW: Nutrition is another phase of the game that has changed significantly over the years. Nutrition is of the utmost importance right now. Eating healthy meals is encouraged. We also have come to realize over the years that you're going to burn out if you don't eat breakfast. You need to eat breakfast, which a lot of guys used to not do. Then, throughout the day, drink a lot of water. You have to take in your fluids to avoid leg cramps.

Maxey, who also works with players on their eating habits, is big into carbohydrates and proteins. You need to have your fruits and vegetables, but you also have to get your proteins. Tim puts the guys on a well-rounded program. He doesn't actually tell them what to eat when the season is over, but he makes suggestions, and they weigh in periodically to see where their weight is.

In general, not only in baseball, good nutrition is extremely important. What you eat determines how you feel and dictates your recovery. Nutrition is one aspect of baseball that is still growing in terms of what we're learning every day. Back in the early days of baseball there was the Babe Ruth diet, which consisted of a hot dog (or several) and a beer (or a six-pack). Times have changed dramatically. Today, many players are very nutrition-oriented and are fueling their bodies like they should in order to perform at a top level everyday. A baseball player always wants to have an edge over his opponent. Nutrition is one area where you can improve to help with recovery and get that extra edge.

MAXEY'S MAXIMS

Technique is the first casualty of fatigue.

EATING FOR ENERGY FROM TIM MAXEY

TM: With all of the traveling and the food supplied in clubhouses, it takes a lot of discipline for a major league player to stay consistent with his diet during the season. Even though players are getting paid to be at the top of their performance for 162 games a year, all of us should strive for good nutrition. We emphasize that our players need two quality meals before they come to work. For a night game that starts at 7:05, some players get to the stadium around 2:30 in the afternoon. So even though our baseball schedule is almost like working the second shift, we want the players to have two good meals before they get to the "office."

Why two quality meals? Your body's going to draw energy from what it's been given on that day. If you have enough energy, obviously you're going to feel like performing better. It doesn't mean you're going to execute better—you have to do the execution—but your body will be better prepared to do the execution.

I strongly encourage players to avoid sweets as much as possible, along with fried foods and sodas. Those all provide useless calories. If you can avoid those, you'll end up keeping off a lot of excess fat. I emphasize carbohydrates, which are what your muscles and your brain use for energy, in the morning and in the afternoon. Later in the day I recommend more protein. Without a doubt, what you eat and when you eat affect your athletic performance. A wisely selected sports diet helps you feel stronger, train harder and compete better.

MAXEY'S MAXIMS

During training, overload causes the muscle tissue of the body to break down. The body then adapts with two very important factors, nutrition and rest, both of which contribute to the development of new strength. So what you eat before and after training sessions will ultimately determine whether or not your body will adapt to the overload.

LOW CARBS/HIGH PROTEIN OR HIGH CARBS/LOW PROTEIN?

We hear a lot of buzzwords today about low-carbohydrate/high-protein diets. We've had a lot of players who could not perform, energy-wise, on high-protein diets. People might try to tell you that cutting out your carbohydrates and consuming a lot of protein will help you feel better, but I'm here to tell you that it doesn't work, and I have several examples.

Your activity level dictates where your carbohydrate level should be. If you aren't very active, you don't need as many carbohydrates. If you're extremely active, like a professional baseball player who takes batting practice in the afternoon, plays a game at night, then lifts weights, your energy expenditure will be high. You have to fuel that energy through the body. Your body will use those carbohydrates for energy, because that is the preferred source of fuel for the muscles.

Even when the body is able to use fat effectively as an energy source, high-intensity strength training and conditioning will demand energy at too fast a rate for fat or protein to be the only sources utilized. Only carbohydrate energy will be broken down fast enough.

JUICERS NEED NOT APPLY

Lifting, conditioning and good nutrition will enhance your performance—not popping, swallowing, mixing, stirring or injecting. Certain supplements, when combined with well-balanced meals, are beneficial to the training athlete. In fact, without question, athletes who train hard need extra nutrients. That means supplements, not steroids. Steroids do not help your performance on the field. Forget the 70-plus medical reasons for not taking steroids, far too many athletes believe now in supplementing with extra protein instead of messing with chemically altering their bodies. Sure, you will get muscles to "swell" with steroids, but your tendons don't adapt to the stress of lifting.

IN THE LONG-TERM, STEROIDS ARE NOT WORTH IT!

SPORTS NUTRITION TIPS

The following tips are taken from the Cleveland Indians Strength and Conditioning manual that Tim Maxey gives each of the players.

1. Drink at least eight 12-ounce glasses of water per day.

2. Drink juices instead of sweetened fluids. Fruit juices contain more carbohydrates than sport or soft drinks, and offer important nutrients that contribute to growth and maintenance of muscle, cartilage and bone.

3. Eating more small meals rather than fewer large meals, will keep your metabolism at a consistent rate all day and allow you to burn more calories.

4. Be sure breakfast is your largest meal of the day, with each additional meal tapering down to where dinner is your smallest (and lowest in carbohydrates) meal of the day.

5. Eat protein with each meal.

6. Carbohydrates supply the body with the energy that it needs. Your best energy sources come from carbs such as rice, and fruits, like oranges and bananas.

7. Steam, boil or grill vegetables; broil, bake or grill meats.

8. Eat a variety of fruits, vegetables, nuts and seeds to ensure that you are getting valuable vitamins and minerals necessary for recovery and function during intense training.

9. If possible, eat low-fat foods and avoid all fried foods.

10. Weight loss and weight gain are nothing more than intake versus expenditure. If you burn more calories than you consume, weight loss will occur. If you intake more calories than you burn, weight gain will occur, but it will be muscular in nature with strength training and quality food choices.

Conclusion

FW: Conditioning and nutrition programs, such as those you've seen in this chapter, are vital in the success of today's baseball player. Times have changed. Players in the 1970s and '80s tended to put on more weight—and not the good kind—as the season progressed, through "only" playing baseball and eating more food. We would be out after a game eating hamburgers and drinking milkshakes. Today's players stay balanced throughout the season, and generally eat better than we did, even though those hamburgers and milkshakes did taste pretty good. We certainly didn't lift weights during the season, and we didn't have a structured off-season program, so we tended to get fatigued when the weather got really hot later in the summer.

I think baseball players today are in much better shape physically than when I played. I'm convinced that that can be attributed directly to conditioning and nutrition programs and philosophies similar to what we outlined in this chapter. With similar programs, players today are able to stay stronger longer and have more stamina toward the end of the season. Even though you may have other activities happening during your off season, or you can't adhere to a strict in-season conditioning program, find a workout that works for you in improving your baseball play, and stay as consistent as possible. Your baseball career may benefit from it.

MAXEY'S MAXIMS

Training Hard + Eating Right = Positive Results

MAXEY'S MAXIMS

STRENGTH AND CONDITIONING GOALS
—Improve athletic performance on the field.
—Aggressive prevention of injuries.
—Reach individual full potential.

Chapter 7

MTXE: Mental Toughness Xtra Effort

Former New York Yankee catcher Yogi Berra is widely known for what are called "Yogi-isms," profound statements he has made through the years that don't always make the most sense...well, maybe they do make some logical sense. Two of the most popular "Yogi-isms" are "How can you think and hit at the same time?" and "Baseball is ninety percent mental. The other half is physical." Those two quotations tie in perfectly with the mental aspect of baseball.

There are many baseball movements that probably are best done by second nature, instead of thinking too much. At the same time, however, baseball is a game of the mind, especially when you look at a duel between a pitcher and a hitter (although I don't know many people that would agree with Yogi's 90 percent mental and 50 percent physical statement). Still, baseball is more mental than physical, and the players who quickly realize that and can grasp what to do and what not to do will end up playing the game a long time very successfully. The basis for this chapter is from a widely used phrase: Mental Toughness Extra Effort—MTXE. The term was brought to the forefront by former Wichita State University men's basketball coach Gene Smithson in the 1980s. MTXE became a battle call for many of Smithson's Shocker teams that included former National Basketball Association star, Xavier McDaniel. MTXE certainly can be applied to most areas of baseball and life.

The mental side of baseball

Let's face it, baseball can be a boring game to spectators. It's not like football, where there is hard hitting on every play. It's not like basketball where the action is fast and furious, back and forth, most of the time. If you're a thinking man, then baseball is the best for you. As I mentioned in chapter one, baseball is like chess or checkers or backgammon.

Baseball is a thinking man's game. Before every pitch as a defensive player, you look at the game's situation and the hitter to anticipate who the hitter is, the type of hitter he is, what he's trying to do, then you counteract that with your defensive moves. As a hitter, you're working against the pitcher and catcher, trying to out-think them. The pitcher and catcher are trying to out-think the hitter. Those things make the game what it is. That's why, when you're successful in a particular situation, your chest swells up in pride. You won that battle.

You especially need smart thinkers up the middle on defense, because those positions can't be run from the bench. Those players must determine who's going to cover second base on a steal or a double-play situation. Those players have to know the hitter, the situation, the count, and the tendencies of the other team on certain counts. A great thinker up the middle at the professional level is Roberto Alomar, who broke the record for most Gold Gloves by an American League second baseman.

Baseball is like solving a problem. Think about being in a classroom and the feeling you have when you correctly answer a difficult math problem or science question. That's the feeling you want to have in baseball. You have to react to what you see and what you know when you're playing baseball. You have to be a great anticipator of what's happening in front of you. Great players come from that mold. As a thinking baseball player, you are trying to take advantage of the other team's lack of ability to think. In a game during the 2001 season between the Royals and the Indians, Kenny Lofton was on first for Cleveland. On a ball that was lined to Royals' left fielder Dee Brown, Lofton took a wide turn around second base. Brown immediately came up and threw to second, thinking he had Lofton hung out to dry. When the throw went toward

Jonathan Daniel/Getty Images

Kenny Lofton

second, Lofton took off for third and was safe. Lofton out-thought Brown that time. In that situation, the outfielder should wait and make the runner, who is in no man's land, commit to a base before making a throw. That's why I tell base runners to run with their heads up and their ears open. On defense you need to play with your head up and your eyes open. Lofton has out-thought a lot of major-league players. He is a smart, complete baseball player.

MY BEST ADVICE

"Keep the game simple. Learn the simple things first. Don't bypass something that seems simple just because you think you know it.
The mental approach and the challenge of fundamental baseball, along with simple teaching points, will start to formulate a necessary fundamental foundation."
—*Tony Muser, former major-league infielder, and current coach*

THE DAILY APPROACH

Several changes have affected the game of baseball through the years, but one aspect that has not changed much is the mental approach. Most players still get ready for the game the same way, with the belief that they want to win the game. You prepare yourself the best you can for that particular day.

Part of that preparation needs to be in your attitude. You need to have a strong, positive attitude going into every game. That positive attitude comes from what you know about the people you are going to play against. The more information you have, the more confident you're going to be. Today's player is more prepared than at any other time in the history of the game. At the major league level today, players are supplied with more visual information to help them learn almost everything about the people they're competing against. The vast information available today has helped a player's mental approach because it gives him additional confidence. For any player at any level, though, positive attitude comes from self-confidence. If you have confidence in what you can do as a player and confidence in your knowledge of your opponent, then it all comes together.

MY BEST ADVICE

"Don't ever let anybody tell you what you can't do, or what position you can't play. I've played shortstop all my life, but a lot of people told me that I couldn't play short because of my size and because I didn't have a strong arm. Always trust your abilities, and never give up."
—*Omar Vizquel, shortstop*

In addition to a positive attitude, the more relaxed you can be on the field, the better off you're going to be. If you're tight (physically and mentally), your body is not going to function smoothly for you. It's not going to react to situations with the response time that you would like. You're always going to be a few steps behind. Just relax and let everything develop in front of you, then react to it.

STAYING FOCUSED ON DEFENSE

Players at all levels often make defensive errors because they lose their focus, even on what should be a routine play. To help prevent it from happening to you, always remember this one simple rule: concentration is required on every pitch. Period. If you have concentration on every pitch that is made to the plate, then you're going to have concentration on the ball if it's hit in your direction. You have to expect the ball to be hit to you on every pitch. It all starts with concentration on the player with the ball—the pitcher—focusing on each pitch that he releases to the plate.

Concentrating on every pitch really wasn't difficult for me to learn to do. When you strive to be the best player you can be, regardless of where you are in your baseball "career," you are required to concentrate. I always felt that if I didn't concentrate, and a ball got by me that shouldn't have gotten by, or I bobbled a ball that shouldn't have been bobbled, I was letting the pitcher down. It takes a lot of effort to pitch. When a guy makes a good pitch and gets the batter to hit a "routine" ground ball to you, you have to make that play. I came up in an era where that was your territory, your job. If I didn't get it done, I was letting my teammates down, and I was letting the pitcher down on that particular day.

MY BEST ADVICE:

"A game can be won or lost in any inning and on any one pitch. As a defensive player, you need to be ready on every pitch. As an offensive player, you need to watch each pitch so that it can prepare you for that one moment when you have a chance to contribute. There is a value with concentrating, being engaged, on every pitch offensively and defensively."
——*Cal Ripken Jr., one of the best "gamers" I've ever known*

BATTLING THE DREADED HITTING SLUMP

As a player or a coach, you need to understand that every baseball player is going to face an offensive slump at some point in his career. *Every* player. A slump is more dramatic for a major leaguer than for an amateur because of the importance that is put on it. A kid not getting a base hit is only tormented, whereas a professional's livelihood is on the line. The big difference is that if the young kid stays in a slump, and a coach or parent is not careful, the kid will quit playing; whereas the professional has to find a way to hit. Therefore, the major leaguer has to keep working, keep digging, keep going up to the plate, and keep working on his trade. Sooner or later, he usually comes around. I think that same philosophy can be applied to the little league hitter who is in a slump. Don't give up. The one thing to keep in mind constantly during a hitting slump is that you're going to get a hit.

Different factors can result in a hitting slump. One of the main reasons that a player will go into a slump is a lack of work. A player can go into a slump because of a failure to pay attention, or a lack of a plan when he goes to the plate, or a lack of a routine before a game to keep his swing together. A lack of preparation and work will put you in a slump in a hurry.

Sometimes a player forces himself into a slump when he's actually on the verge of a great streak. This is the player who is swinging the bat well and hitting balls hard, but they're being caught. That player might have a tendency to swing the bat harder, and the next thing he knows, he's 0-for-16.

The scariest and loneliest place for a hitter in a slump is being too slow for the fastball and too quick for the breaking ball. That's no man's land. If you're swinging at strikes and hitting the ball squarely on the nose, but the defense is making the plays, there's not much you can do about it. That's not a slump; that's just bad luck.

However, if you are taking strikes and swinging at balls, or not striking the ball cleanly, then you're in a slump. In that situation, you're not seeing the ball, and you're not being patient enough to let the ball get to you to make sure it's a strike. Oftentimes when you go into a slump, you start pulling your head and your front shoulder. At that point, you have obviously lost your focus.

When you're not hitting the ball hard, popping up balls, hitting weak grounders, swinging at bad pitches and striking out, then you're not seeing the ball and you're not concentrating; you're in a slump. That's why many managers, when someone's not swinging the bat well, will put on a hit and run. By putting on a hit and run, the hitter is forced to protect a runner, so he has to concentrate a little bit more and try to hit the ball hard on the ground to the shortstop or second baseman.

The best advice I ever received about working through a slump came from Hal McRae. When I first came up to the majors, he told me, "Hey, the tougher things get, the more aggressive you have to get, because sometimes when you go in a slump you tend to shrink. The more you shrink back, the harder it is to come out again. You still have to be yourself and you have to be aggressive at the plate. The key thing is to make sure that you're swinging at strikes and not balls."

It is tough to keep that slump out of your mind, but you have to keep working. You have to go up to the plate relaxed. (Remember that being tense only creates more problems.) Stay focused and stay positive.

BE A TEAM PLAYER

It's interesting to listen to teams that are playing well and notice how the word "chemistry" always comes up. That chemistry—playing well together and having an idea of what each of your teammates can and will do on the field—is what ushers in a good team morale. Team chemistry or morale doesn't mean that you have to be best friends with all of your teammates off the field. Our championship Royals teams had good on-the-field chemistry but we didn't all hang out together away from the stadium. That was fine. The championship Yankees teams of the 1970s were infamous for their disagreements off the field. That was fine. Even though you don't have to be best friends with all your teammates, you should respect each of them and encourage them on the field.

When teams are losing, the morale is a lot lower, and there doesn't seem to be much chemistry. From the players' standpoint, that's when you have to keep pumping each other up to boost each other's confidence and be good support for each other. Otherwise, it's tough to bring back that morale.

Staying positive... in baseball and in life

Life and sport are usually different, but the positive approach applies to both. A positive attitude comes from wanting to be the best at what you do, regardless of what that is. You need to believe in yourself to be the best at what you do. That's where my positive attitude came from. I wanted to be the best second baseman in the American League. I wanted to be the best second baseman in all of baseball, for that matter. When you decide something like that, you have to go out and approach it with that attitude.

As my kids have grown up, I have tried to teach them to stay positive in everything that they do. I don't know if you can actually teach kids that, but as a coach or parent you should encourage kids to do the best they can do. Each of us should always give our best effort in all that we do. If we fall short, that's OK, because we gave it our best. We can't all be number one, but we can all do the best with the job that is handed to us. If giving our best is all that we can do, then that's all we can do. My dad told me a long time ago, "You can only get so much out of a body every day. Eventually you've got to shut her down, come back the next day and start all over again." Make the most of your body's best each day.

Baseball teaches us many of life's lessons about a myriad of topics including teamwork and competition. It also teaches us how to stay positive, how to battle through the tough times, and how important it is to always try our hardest. Whatever you're doing, in life or in baseball, give it all you've got for as long as you can and see what great things happen.

WHITE'S WORDS OF WISDOM

- If you're not willing to give your best effort in baseball, you shouldn't play at all. That's the same with life. You need to be willing to live it to the fullest and be the best you can be at everything you do.
- If you have talent and you don't use that talent to be the best of your ability, you're not only frustrating yourself, but you're frustrating the people who are trying to help you. A great example is a mom or a dad with a talented kid who won't give his best effort to bring it out, so mom and dad get frustrated because they don't know how to get the best out of him.
- Success starts from within. If you want to be successful, then oftentimes you can make that happen.
- You can only play sports for a certain amount of time. If you don't give your best effort, before you know it, you're going to run out of time and wish that you had given it your all.

Chapter 8

Putting it all Together

Before you go out and apply everything that you've learned from this book, I want to offer you some "fatherly" advice and address a couple of issues that I'm often asked about that affect baseball today.

OPTIONS, OPTIONS AND MORE OPTIONS

Times have changed for kids quite a bit through the years. It used to be common to see fields and playgrounds filled with kids playing ball after school and throughout the summer months. Kids would be outside in droves playing whatever sport was in season. I noticed a few years ago that fields and parks weren't as full as they were in the "good old days." In the neighborhood where I grew up, when it was baseball season, everybody played baseball. When it was football season, everybody played football. When it was basketball season, everybody played basketball. We enjoyed playing sports.

During the summer, as soon as our parents went to work in the mornings, we went down to a park and played baseball for three or four hours before having to go back home to finish our chores. We looked forward to doing that each day. If we couldn't get to the park, we'd play in our neighborhood. In those instances, we hung a piece of tin with some string from the garage, then used a tennis ball and a broom handle (for the bat) and played ball. We used the sound of the tin to determine whether or not the pitch was a strike.

It's amazing how inventive you can be when you really want to do something. My sisters used to get dolls at Christmas. Since we couldn't afford baseballs, we waited until my sisters had combed all the hair out of their dolls and weren't playing with them anymore, and then we would take the heads off, stuff them with rags, and wrap them with duct tape. Those made great balls.

The local elementary school had a field marked for softball, so we sometimes went up there and played with a baseball. When the stitching came off the few baseballs we did have, we took black electrical tape and wrapped up the ball so we could keep playing. There were ways to get done what we felt we had to get done. We improvised as much as we could. Today, we don't see as many kids going out on their own and doing those types of things. And that's not necessarily a reflection on the kids. Today, things are so controlled by the local park departments with various softball and baseball leagues that kids oftentimes get run off the field.

At the same time, even though I miss seeing kids out playing ball, I have to admit that I think it's better today. It's important for everyone to have choices. For us there were really only three sports options: basketball, baseball and football. Today, more and more high school athletes are training year-round for the main three sports in addition to other options such as soccer, tennis, swimming, track and field, and boxing.

Thinking back, some of the guys in my old neighborhood who weren't very good at sports ended up watching from the sidelines. If the games weren't serious we would include those guys, but when the competition heated up, they were back on the sidelines. For instance, my brother was too small to play football, but he loved to play in the park. He couldn't play in high school, so he became the student-manager of the team just to be close to the game. There are many more opportunities for them to be competitive and stay athletic.

There certainly weren't enough choices for kids to be active mentally in some sort of game. Our main thinking games were checkers, backgammon and dominoes, where some of those other kids who were on the sidelines during athletic competition could compete pretty well. Today's kids have many more high-tech mental outlets such as computers and handheld games.

Today's kids have many great opportunities to be well rounded in their sports and academics.

FOREVER AMERICA'S PASTIME

Fortunately, one sport that can be played or practiced year-round is baseball. Cities have indoor batting cages and other facilities where kids can go during the off season and get instruction on hitting and fielding. Despite that option, however, I think the overall athletic choices that are available today have hurt baseball more so than the other sports. The talent is still there, but today's players are multi-talented. Unless Major League Baseball teams grab these kids out of high school and offer them enough money, these athletes will probably pick college to play another sport.

Not many colleges offer full scholarships in baseball, so many of those multi-sport players play another sport that may offer more money for school, such as basketball or football. Sometimes those athletes will come back to baseball—Deion Sanders, Bo Jackson, Brian Jordan—after focusing on their main sport from college. Players love baseball, but the money isn't always there for them to pursue the sport out of high school.

Baseball is something that everyone grows up with. At one time, it was the number-one sport in America. The first thing that dads usually bought for their kids was a glove and a baseball, rather than a football or basketball. Kids would play catch in their backyards or at the parks. With the influences of players from places like Latin America (Sammy Sosa, for instance) and Japan (Ichiro Suzuki), baseball is gaining more worldwide popularity and continues to be a great game, but it's losing popularity here.

MY ADVICE? HAVE FUN AND LOVE THE GAME

I'm often asked what it takes to be a major-league prospect. It takes good speed, a strong throwing arm, great hitting ability, and strong defensive skills. In order to accomplish those things, becoming a prospect takes playing a lot of baseball. Play as much baseball as you can. Learn to love the game. Learn to have fun in the game. At the same time, when you decide you want to play this game for a living, prepare yourself in two ways—if you make it, and if you don't make it. Prepare yourself so that if you don't make it, your second choice will be just as rewarding as if you were a Major League Baseball player.

I always loved baseball. My dad, who had played for Memphis in the Negro Leagues, helped fuel my passion. The fun part of baseball for me was when it was fun for everybody on the team. Early in life Dad taught me how to truly enjoy the game.

When I was 12 years old I was playing on the best baseball team in our league. Maybe I should take out the word "playing." I was sitting on the bench—I wasn't playing. Still, our team was winning. During our fourth game of the season, my dad came and got me off the bench. He was pulling me from the team. I left that field kicking and screaming, literally. When we got home and I had stopped crying, I asked Dad why he took me off the team. He told me that if I wanted to be a baseball player, then I had to play baseball. He said, "You can't learn baseball when you're sitting on the bench."

Dad put me on the last-place team. I couldn't believe it! One minute I was deciding where I was going to put my first-place trophy with that other team, and the next minute I was on our league's worst team. Dad told me, "If you're going to play this game, then you have to learn how to enjoy this game. The only way you learn how to enjoy this game is to play the game." We didn't win on the last-place team, but I played every game. That was probably the best learning experience I could have received.

Because of that lesson, I have a tough time watching these really good athletes who could go to one university and play all four years, opt for a high-profile school where they might sit on the bench for two years then possibly play their last two years. I haven't been able to figure that one out. Those two years of not playing don't improve the player's ability, because he's not competing every day.

It doesn't matter where you play baseball in college, or high school for that matter. If you're a talented player, the scouts are going to see you. You would be much better off going to a smaller school and playing four years, constantly honing your baseball skills. Have fun and love the game.

MY BEST ADVICE ABOUT BEING A PROSPECT

"A big criteria to being a prospect is running speed. How fast do you run the 60? Also, how good of a throwing arm do you have? You need to learn how to develop your arm and body to become a baseball player. You have to swing the bat for hours and hours. If you're a pitcher, you have to condition yourself to pitch. If you can't do those things, you might as well go on to something else."
—*Syd Thrift, a long-time baseball coach, scout and executive, and the director of the former Royals Baseball Academy*

SPEAKING OF COLLEGE...
BE PREPARED BEFORE YOU JUMP

I understand that with the money available today, it's tough to convince college players to stay in school instead of turning pro in the main three sports. Added to that difficult argument is the fact that a lot of kids don't come from a background where they have that type of money in their family. Kids, especially from low-income areas, have so much responsibility to help their family when they rise to that level. The first thing they want to do is buy their mom a house and their dad a car, and take care of their brothers and sisters.

Some people don't understand that responsibility because they haven't faced it. My agent, for instance, grew up with two parents who were accountants, his brother is a lawyer and he's a lawyer—there was never really a need financially for him or his brother to take care of anyone else in that family. I have four sisters and a brother, and I was the only person who made a significant amount of money in the family. Therefore, over the years I've tried to help them out as much as possible. I don't have a problem with that, nor do I have any type of ill feelings toward people who don't have to face that issue. That's just the way it is.

So how do you convince these athletes that turning pro early is not the best thing to do? I'm not sure that they should be convinced. I like former North Carolina basketball coach Dean Smith's analogy when asked about his players leaving school early for the NBA. He has replied by asking that if a person's son or daughter was a journalism student, a junior, and a publication such as the *Wall Street Journal* came along and offered that child $5 million to leave school and work full-time, what would the parent tell them to do? Would he want the child to skip the money to finish school, or take the job and finish school at a later time? The obvious answer is to take the job with the paper.

However, if you are one of those rare athletes, or the parent of one of those athletes thinking of leaving school early, be forewarned. The first thing to do before declaring for the draft is to make sure that you're definitely going to get drafted, because once you leave you can't go back to college and play. Be absolutely sure.

Another thing to keep in mind is how well you prepare yourself academically before your junior year. If you prepare yourself well academically and opt to leave early, but you don't get drafted, you can at least go back to school and finish. If you pin all of your hopes on making it in professional sports—MLB, NFL or NBA—and you don't make it, you're going to have problems going back to school.

If you're still in high school and have thought about dropping out, don't. Remember that you have to finish high school before a major league team can draft you. Kids need to stay in school from the first through the 12th grade, and then continue their formal education as much as possible.

You should strive to be a student for the rest of your life. Try to constantly learn, even if it's not in a school setting. Stay in good health by avoiding drugs, guns and gang activities, or whatever may keep you from obtaining your goals in life. Combining good health and education is a must for any child to succeed. My motto is "Be a student first."

Goals

It's important for all of us—including kids—to set goals. We can set goals in athletics. We can set goals in school or work. We can set goals in life. There really aren't many areas where we can't set goals. The problem some people face in setting goals is that they aim only for the maximum. That's great, but unrealistic goals are not good without a plan of action.

You need to set intermediate goals. Where do you want to be in 30 days? In 60 days? In 90 days? Rather than saying that you want to hit .300 this season with a ton of home runs and runs batted in, set short-term goals to help reach the end result. If you don't set reachable goals throughout the season to get to that one ultimate goal at the end of year, and you fall short by two home runs, you'll feel that you didn't accomplish your goal. If you set intermediate goals, you can track your progress and feel good about what you're accomplishing because you'll realize that you're working toward the end goal.

Setting and achieving goals is hard work. Many people like long-range goals better than short-term ones. But before you reach that end result, you have to put in a lot of hard work. When it's all said and done, however, you will know what hard work it took to reach your goals. That personal satisfaction can be very rewarding.

MY BEST ADVICE

"My philosophy is simple. You're only going to get out of something what you put into it. If you don't put anything into it, you shouldn't expect anything in return. There are no shortcuts to success—there has to be some blood, some sweat and some tears."
—*Ozzie Smith, Hall of Fame shortstop*

AP/WWP

DECIDE FOR YOURSELF

Whenever my kids ask for my advice, I offer it, but I always tell them to make their own decisions. They shouldn't make decisions based on my life, or what I've done. They should make decisions based on their families and what they want to try to get done. That should apply to all of us. We need to make our decisions based on our personal goals and beliefs.

Finally...

DO THE RIGHT THING

Growing up, you have a tendency to see a lot of things through your friends' eyes. You know the people whom you hang out with who are doing the good things; and you know the kids who are doing the bad things. You have to be able to make a decision about all of that and the type of person or player you want to be. Then you have to make a commitment to be that person. Sometimes, making a commitment to be something different than the norm is not very easy to do. If you stay firm, you can be what you want to be.

We always hear stories from major-league players about how they were pretty good growing up, but they knew guys who were better players. They will usually tell how the more talented players were involved with chasing girls, or drinking alcohol, or doing drugs, or doing something else that didn't allow them to pursue their talents, and they didn't succeed in baseball. Whereas the major-league player who wasn't as talented but led a straight life, worked hard and reached his goal.

I grew up around gangs, but I never participated in them because baseball is what I wanted to do. I knew people in gangs, but all I wanted to do was play baseball. I did whatever I needed to do to stay off the streets. I was home at night. I went fishing and hunting with my dad. I played sports.

You have to be able to separate yourself from the bad influences, but first you have to decide what type of person you are and what you want out of life. That usually comes from how well your parents have done raising you, and how good you feel about yourself. I was blessed because caring parents raised me.

If you're serious about being a baseball player—or a teacher, or a doctor, or a writer, or whatever—you should focus. Apply yourself. Be the best person you can be. Stay off drugs. Avoid violence and gangs. Study. Remember what Abraham Lincoln said: "I will study and I will prepare; and perhaps someday my chance will come."

MY BEST ADVICE

"As a baseball player, you must keep your eyes open and be willing to learn, and be willing to practice, and be willing to experiment with ways to improve your game. To be a successful baseball player, you have to continually try to learn. If you can learn one thing every day about the game of baseball—rules, technique, whatever—you can learn a heck of a lot."
—*Jamie Moyer, pitcher, who, from 1996-2000, had the major league's third-highest winning percentage (.673)*

As I mentioned in the first chapter, one of my goals with this book is to give you tools that you can use to become a better baseball player. Obviously, I can't guarantee that you'll reach the major leagues if you follow everything in this book. However, I can guarantee that if you apply the fundamentals that you've learned, and you work at those skills, you can become the best baseball player that your abilities will allow.

Now, get out there and enjoy this great game of baseball...the greatest game in the world.

FRANK WHITE

Frank White was an eight-time winner of the Rawlings Gold Glove Award and five-time All-Star during his 18-year career at second base for the Kansas City Royals, as they went to six American League Championship Series and two World Series, including the championship season of 1985. White finished with a .983 career fielding percentage during those 18 seasons.

Offensively, White collected 2,006 hits and batted .255 in 2,324 games. He is the only second baseman besides Jackie Robinson to bat cleanup in the World Series. White also was the MVP of the 1980 ALCS. In 1995, he was inducted into the Royals Hall of Fame and had his No. 20 retired.

Since retiring in 1990, White has coached in the Boston Red Sox and Royals organizations. He spent two seasons in the Royals front office as a special assistant to the general manager, before becoming the manager of the club's Class AA affiliate in Wichita, Kansas, in 2004.

White, who has four children, lives in the Kansas City area with his wife, Teresa.

MATT FULKS

Matt Fulks started his journalism career while attending Lipscomb University in Nashville, Tenn., after his baseball career was cut short due to a lack of ability.

Since then he has worked in every form of the media, and now spends his time as a free-lance writer, editor and author. He is a regular contributor to various publications, including *The Kansas City Star* newspaper. He is the author/co-author of seven other books, including *Behind the Stats: Tennessee's Coaching Legends*, *The Road to Canton*, co-authored with NFL Hall of Fame running back Marcus Allen, and *Tales from the Royals Dugout*, co-authored with broadcaster Denny Matthews. Fulks lives in the Kansas City area with his wife, Libby, their children, Helen and Charlie, and their Doberman retriever.

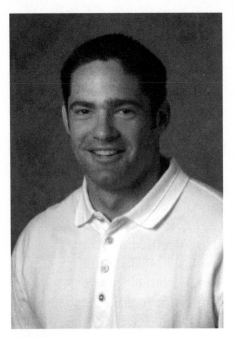

The authors would be remissed if we didn't recognize Tim Maxey, who helped us immensely with chapter 6 on conditioning and nutrition. Maxey, who spent four years as the Royals strength and conditioning coordinator, took a similar position with the Cleveland Indians prior to the 2003 season. Before reaching the major-league level, Maxey was the Royals minor-league strength and conditioning coordinator in 1998 after one year with Class AAA Buffalo in the Indians system. In 1996, Maxey was a graduate strength and conditioning coach at Ohio State University, where he received his Master's Degree. Maxey lives in the Cleveland area with his wife, Amy, and their son, Zachary.